# The Violence of Britishness

# The Violence of Britishness

## Racism, Borders and the Conditions of Citizenship

Nadya Ali

PLUTO PRESS

First published 2023 by Pluto Press
New Wing, Somerset House, Strand, London WC2R 1LA
and Pluto Press, Inc.
1930 Village Center Circle, 3-834, Las Vegas, NV 89134

www.plutobooks.com

British Library Cataloguing in Publication Data
A catalogue record for this book is available from the British Library

ISBN   978 0 7453 4170 5   Paperback
ISBN   978 1 78680 843 1   PDF
ISBN   978 1 78680 844 8   EPUB

This book is printed on paper suitable for recycling and made from fully managed
and sustained forest sources. Logging, pulping and manufacturing processes are
expected to conform to the environmental standards of the country of origin.

Typeset by Stanford DTP Services, Northampton, England

Simultaneously printed in the United Kingdom and United States of America

# Contents

# Abbreviations

| | |
|---|---|
| BBR | British Bill of Rights |
| BNP | British National Party |
| CC | Charity Commission |
| CCT | Commonwealth Citizen's Taskforce |
| ECHR | European Convention on Human Rights |
| EDL | English Defence League |
| EHRC | Equality and Human Rights Commission |
| FGM | Female Genital Mutilation |
| GFC | Global Financial Crisis |
| HBA | Honour Based Abuse |
| HRA | Human Rights Act |
| ICS | Indian Civil Servant |
| ILR | Indefinite Leave to Remain stamp |
| IS | Islamic State |
| JCWI | Joint Council for the Welfare of Immigrants |
| LAG | Legal Action Group |
| MATBAPS | The Inter-Ministerial Group on Migrants Access to Benefits and Public Services |
| MINAB | Mosque and Imams National Advisory Board |
| MCB | Muslim Council of Britain |
| NMWAG | National Muslim Women's Advisory Group |
| PCM | National Police Prevent Case Management |
| PD | Prevent Duty |
| PET | Preventing Extremism Together |
| RtR | Right to Rent |
| RtW | Right to Work |
| TPIMs | Terrorism Prevention and Investigation Measures |
| WDL | White Defence League |
| WLLR | Windrush Lesson Learned Review |
| WRAP | Workshop to Raise Awareness of Prevent |

# Acknowledgements

I would like to thank David Shulman at Pluto Press for his patience, support and enthusiasm for this book. We first spoke about a potential project in 2017, which now feels like another world ago. The ideas in this book began to take form over twelve years ago in my PhD supervised by Andreas Behnke, whose teaching and conversation sparked my own intellectual journey and a cherished friendship.

A huge thank you to Alan Lester for his time and intellectual generosity in sharing his expertise on British colonial history which formed the basis for revisions to various chapters. I would like to acknowledge Gargi Bhattacharyya, Louiza Odysseos and Robbie Shilliam for their comments on early drafts of the book proposal and their scholarship, which guided my inquiries. I also thank my former colleagues and friends in the department of International Relations at the University of Sussex, where I developed many of the ideas set out in this book.

To my comrades at Sussex UCU – especially Malcolm James, Sam Solomon and Arabella Stanger – while I may no longer be on the picket line with you, I will always carry the hope generated by collective action in my heart. I also want to thank Shereen Fernandez, Naaz Rashid, Rizwaan Sabir and Waqas Tufail whose scholarship has illuminated mine. Their camaraderie and fierce example enables me to keep writing critically about Prevent and Muslim life, even when the costs of doing so have felt very high.

To friends and family who enrich my life and deepen the joy and comfort this world has to offer, here's looking at you: Nicola Abram, Lizzie Barker, Adam Beach, Dan Bulley, Synne Dyvik, Riz Khan, Corinne Heaven, Oriana Pagano, Norma Rossi, Malte Riemann, Brett Mills, Neelam Mills, Beth Summers, Vicki Sutton, Jon Traynor, and David Yuratich. A special mention also for Lucy Flowerdew, Jamie Whitham, John Whitham and Trish Whitham. I also thank my instructor Dave Courtney Jones and my siblings at Tiger Crane Kung Fu, without whom I would just think of myself as a floating head rather than a body in the world.

I owe a particular debt to my sisters in struggle Akanksha Mehta, Althea Maria Rivas and Bal Sokhi-Bulley: thank you for seeing me and for helping me to see. To my nieces and nephews Sahil, Amman, Imaan, Zahra, Hina, Laibah, Eshaan, Yusuf and Sawera, this one's for you. To Farah and Naveed, my kith, my kin, I hope this is not too boring a read. Last but not least, to Ben Whitham who has brightened every day, weathered every storm and taken such care of the dreams I spread under his feet, thank you for treading so softly.

This book is dedicated to the victims and survivors of border violence, wherever in the world they may be.

Together, we bear witness.

# Introduction:
# Undeserving Citizens

We are still a long way from comprehending why Britain has shown itself to be incapable of coming to terms with its black and other minority settlers, why it has been quite so hopeless and resistant to the possibility of adjusting that imperilled national identity so that it might be more inclusive, cosmopolitan and habitable.

Paul Gilroy[1]

In 2015, three 15-year-old friends from East London, Shamima Begum, Khadiza Sultana and Amira Abase, left their homes in order to travel to Islamic State-controlled territory. Unbeknownst to the trio, they were being assisted in their travel by an agent working in the employ of Canadian intelligence services, who was expediting their journey to underage marriage, injury and death.[2] The friends were among the estimated 5000 Europeans who migrated from their homes to the newly founded caliphate spanning Northern Syria and Iraq.[3] Four years later, with the Islamic State vanquished, Sultana was reported to have died in a bombing – while Abase's fate is unknown. However, it was Begum who dominated the headlines in Britain. In 2019, the heavily pregnant teenager gave an interview to UK Sky News from a refugee camp in Syria. She asked to be allowed to return to Britain for the sake of her unborn child.

The then home secretary Sajid Javid responded by revoking her British citizenship and effectively making her stateless, a practice which is illegal under international law. In a subsequent appeal against the decision, judges argued that Begum was 'Bangladeshi by descent' according to Bangladeshi nationality law and not at risk of statelessness.[4] However, this assertion was contested by Begum's legal representation on the basis that Bangladesh carries the death sentence for terrorism offences, for which she could be prosecuted upon arrival. The ruling effectively forced Begum to choose between an uncertain future in a refugee camp, or a potential death sentence in Bangladesh. Despite protestations that she had been groomed by IS and trafficked as a child, Begum was cast as a national traitor by the press and politicians, where her age was immaterial in the face of the offences she was thought to have committed. A month after her citizenship was revoked, Begum's newborn son Jarrah died in al-Roj camp. He was her third child who had died, all of whom were British citizens.

In 2018, at the same time that questions around the future of Britain's Muslims in Syria were being debated, the so-called 'Windrush scandal' broke. It emerged that the Home Office had deported, detained, made jobless, homeless and denied life-saving access to healthcare to 'countless' numbers of British citizens from Commonwealth countries who could not provide evidence of their immigration status. Coverage of this scandal focused primarily on the Windrush generation, or those who had travelled from the Caribbean to Britain after the Second World War. In reality, those with Indian, Nigerian, Ghanaian, Pakistani and Bangladeshi heritage were also affected by the Windrush scandal. One such case was that of 58-year-old David Jameson, who came to the UK from Jamaica as a child on his grandmother's passport in 1966.

According to UK immigration law, those like Jameson who arrived before 1973 are entitled to indefinite leave to remain as Commonwealth citizens.[5] But, unable to provide paperwork to substantiate the date of his arrival and under increasingly punitive immigration rules, Jameson was fired from his construction job for failing to obtain a National Insurance number. He was then detained at Harmondsworth Immigration Removal Centre where he twice attempted suicide before being deported to Jamaica in 2013. Though he was wrongly deported and is (at the time of writing) homeless, Jameson is not entitled to help that has been made available for other victims of the scandal. This was due to a prior criminal conviction for a minor offence from the London riots in 2011, which barred Jameson from accessing assistance.

The treatment of the Windrush generation was attributed to the destruction of landing cards which had provided a historic record of

Commonwealth citizens who had travelled to the UK. However, the Institute of Race Relations (IRR) shows that what happened to Jameson is not an anomaly, but is instead consonant with the broader pattern of aggressive immigration policing affecting British citizens known as the hostile environment.[6] The Immigration Acts of 2014 and 2016 mean that if individuals are unable to provide 'lawful evidence' which proves their settled immigration status, then access to employment, healthcare, welfare benefits, education, housing and banking is denied. Employers, landlords, health practitioners, universities and banks are now legally mandated to carry out immigration checks.

How and why should we think the Windrush scandal alongside the treatment of Britain's Muslims? Understanding how the fate of Shamima Begum, a Muslim child of Bangladeshi immigrants, is connected to that of the Jamaican born David Jameson, who had been resident in the UK since he was a child, is imperative. Both of them are counted among Britain's postcolonial citizens who were born in Britain or have lived here most of their lives, yet neither are considered to be adequately British because they are not white.[7] They are always from somewhere else, usually parts of the former British Empire racialised as not white, to where they can ultimately be 'sent back'. This reality has most recently been embodied in the anti-refugee Borders and Nationality Act (2022) that also allows the British state to deprive Britons of their citizenship without notice. Basit Mahmood argues that 'minorities and those of migrant heritage' are most likely to be targeted by citizenship deprivation, noting that almost 'half of all Asian British people in England and Wales are likely to be eligible (50 per cent), along with two in five black Britons (39 per cent)'.[8] For Frances Webber, the act is also part of a longer trajectory of trying to 'de-nationalise' Muslim citizens in particular.[9]

The idea that 'Britishness' is synonymous with whiteness is rooted in the way we selectively remember and forget histories of British colonialism. Histories of a swashbuckling empire are manifest in this nationalist nostalgia of the present, best exemplified by the politics of Brexit. Postcolonial citizens are viewed as perpetual 'immigrants' and 'minorities' in Britain where the clarion call to *take back control* was at least in part an attempt to pull up the drawbridge and protect what remains of resources that were seen as rightfully belonging to white Britons. Thus, it did not come as a surprise when in June 2022 it emerged that the Home Office had suppressed a report it had commissioned on immigration legislation which argued that 'during the period 1950–81, every single piece of immigration or citizenship legislation was designed at least in part to reduce the number of people with black or brown skin who were permitted to live and work in the UK'.[10]

Nor was it surprising to learn that the Home Office had attempted to 'sanitise' a module designed to teach its employees about 'race, empire and colonialism'.[11] As Jason Arday, who helped design the material, said,

> there seemed to be a reluctance to fully engage with how bad Britain has been in terms of its role in upholding empire and its subsequent hangover. It felt as though the material had been sanitised by civil servants and parliamentarians who did not want to engage with the crux of racism. I felt like we were being asked to engage in historical amnesia.[12]

The attempt to disavow the truth of Britain's racist border policies is part of a longer and more pernicious pattern of colonial amnesia.

*The Violence of Britishness* begins from the premise that counterterrorism and immigration policies are both projects of racial bordering which operate in mutually reinforcing ways to 'keep Britain white'. These policy areas have extended and intensified the way racial borders function formally and informally to exclude postcolonial citizens in the service of an idealised white Britain. The analysis draws on changes in Britain's counter-terrorism apparatus and its immigration regimes since 2010. The first policy to be examined is Prevent, a pre-emptive counter-radicalisation strategy launched as part of the War on Terror, which transformed the relationship between the British state and its Muslim citizens. The book then connects these developments to the emergence of the 'hostile environment', which affects a broader spectrum of the citizens who have historically or more recently come to Britain from parts of its former empire.

What is at stake in thinking about the connections between counter-terrorism and immigration? Prevent and the hostile environment appear to us as very different policy areas which are unconnected to one another. Counter-terrorism seeks to combat political violence perpetrated by non-state actors, whereas immigration regimes decide who can and cannot enter Britain and under what conditions. However, the book shows that counter-terrorism and immigration are policy areas which occupy a common ideological terrain. They arbitrate on what constitutes the white British nation and provide material ways through which the borders of the nation can be understood, enforced, and policed. In other words, the Prevent strategy and the hostile environment are grounded in the racialised struggle over what makes Britain 'British'. The violence of 'Britishness' is therefore the expression of a white national identity that operates to the exclusion of populations who fall outside of this category.

Adopting this perspective forces us to rethink how we can understand the relationship between Britishness, counter-terrorism and immigration. In the overarching context of the politics of Brexit and the politics of austerity, questions about who counts as 'British' and who should enjoy the rights and entitlements of British citizenship are a matter of life and death. The victims of the Windrush scandal who died as a result of the denial of life-saving healthcare, or Muslim children left in unliveable conditions in Syrian camps, exemplify the consequences of being cast out. Questions of national identity are fundamental to how we imagine what Britain is, but more importantly what Britain could be. By prioritising the latter question we can begin to collectively imagine and struggle in the name of a Britain that is not premised on racial, gendered, class and other forms of domination.

To underwrite this point more clearly, in understanding that there are connections between the fate of Britain's Muslims and the Windrush generation (and beyond) means rethinking anti-racist organising against state violence. It is not enough to agitate against Prevent on the one hand without also accounting for how immigration regimes also condemn so many to the misery of racial violence, and vice versa. If we fight for David Jameson because we understand that what has happened to him is a grave injustice, then we must also fight for Shamima Begum and for her three deceased children against this common violence of 'Britishness'.

## Deserving and undeserving citizens?

Thinking about David Jameson and Shamima Begum as equal victims of a border violence enacted in the service of white Britain may 'feel' wrong. This feeling – what scholars describe as an 'affect' – is political, insofar as it is tied to the divergent ways in which those at the centre of counter-terrorism scandals and the Windrush scandal have been mediated for us. Exemplifying this divergence in the *Telegraph* is Leo McKinstry, who writes that Shamima's 'continuing presence in a squalid refugee camp is exactly the punishment she deserves for her collusion with one of the most tyrannical, bloodthirsty organisations that history has known. Whatever the submissive, pleading stance she now adopts, Begum is no victim.'[13]

A *Sun* headline from the same period noted, 'No Regrets; No Remorse; No Entry' as a justification for not bringing Begum home to the UK.[14] The *Metro* meanwhile proclaimed 'Jihadi Bride Wants Baby on NHS', dexterously combining multiple moral panics about 'Jihadi brides', teen pregnancy and health tourism into one headline.[15] For Allison Pearson, again in the *Telegraph*, Shamima's actions betrayed an almost unbearable ingratitude for being born 'in such a country' (Britain) where she benefitted from a free education not available to Muslim girls in other parts of the world.[16]

The food critic, and self-described liberal, Grace Dent argued that Shamima and her friends were an example of 'horror-movie ghouls who hate Britain, gays, democracy, the rights of women and religious freedom.'[17] These framings rendered Shamima an undeserving adult woman – rather than the child she was – and reveal that the entitlements of her citizenship were conditional on her good behaviour. Citizenship was regarded as a gift bestowed upon Shamima by the fair play nation that is Britain, a gift that she failed to adequately appreciate and therefore would now be punished through its removal.

In contrast, the Windrush scandal led to a very public outcry spear-headed by newspapers including the *Daily Mail*, who described it as a 'Fiasco that Shames Britain'.[18] In a letter to the *Independent*, Michael Mann from Shrewsbury wrote about his 'feeling of shame' at the treatment of those victimised by the scandal.[19] Sajid Javid described the Windrush generation as 'outstanding pillars of the community' who 'came to help rebuild this country' after the Second World War.[20] The Windrush generation have come to embody ideas of deserving immigrants: those who have arrived legally and behaved honourably. Unfortunately, this view rests on a particularly egregious denial of the white racial panic in response to post-1945 immigration from the Caribbean, East Africa and South Asia, facilitating acrobatic revisions of British history. The lived reality of the hostile reception which faced black and brown commonwealth subjects upon their arrival in Britain was vicious anti-Black racism and 'Paki' bashing.[21]

Regardless of this pertinent history, images of the SS Empire Windrush arriving at Tilbury docks in 1948 adorned coverage of the scandal. The use of these images represented a backwards glance at a sanitised and romanticised history of misty-eyed migrants from the Caribbean hoping to start a new life in the hallowed streets of the 'motherland'. In the context of these images, feelings of national shame emanate from an understanding of Britain as a fair-minded and tolerant nation which once opened its doors to hardworking immigrants but is now betraying these ideals. The scandal facilitated the resignation of Javid's predecessor, home secretary Amber Rudd over the 'justifiable outrage' surrounding the deportations and the fact that she lied to a Select Committee over the existence of removal targets.[22] The Commonwealth Citizen's Taskforce (CCT) was also established to assist those who had been wrongly affected by legislation ostensibly aimed at undocumented migrants.

Robbie Shilliam has argued that distinctions between who is 'deserving' and who is 'undeserving' are integral to the production of the ongoing racial and class insecurity experienced by postcolonial citizens.[23] He shows how these distinctions emerged from attempts to make hierarchies between diverse populations subjected to British colonial rule.[24] From Manchester, to Bombay, Nairobi and Sydney, the subjects of the British Empire were to be found everywhere from Asia, Africa, North America and Oceania. Theoretically all British subjects, wherever they lived, shared universal rights including the right to enter the United Kingdom. These claims of equality between British subjects in colonies, dominions and mandates were intended to project an idea of imperial unity and underline the liberal character of British colonialism.

In practice this was not the case, however, and there were all kinds of racial, class-based and gendered ways in which the theoretical equality between British subjects was exposed as an exercise in rhetorical piety. For instance, white settler colonies such as Australia, Canada, New Zealand and South Africa agitated to discriminate against British subjects of colour entering these territories through immigration and nationality laws. Similarly, within the UK, degrees of belonging first to the empire and later to the nation were determined by ideas about which subjects were deserving or undeserving depending on the racialized and class characteristics attributed to them.

To bring this back to the present, despite being positioned as either 'deserving' or 'undeserving' both Begum and Jameson remain locked outside of Britain with limited recourse to challenging their removal from the nation. In other words, while one has been cast as a worthy recipient of justice and the other not, the material consequences of being made 'deserving' and 'undeserving' remain surprisingly similar. These equivalent experiences of disentitlement and its harms are further underscored by the Windrush victims continued struggle for justice. For example, in 2021 the *Guardian* reported that the compensation scheme set up to assist victims of Windrush (which cannot be claimed by those with a criminal conviction) has only paid out to 864 of the 15,000 people who were eligible to apply.[25]

Alexandra Ankrah, a Black Home Office employee working on the compensation scheme, resigned in protest at the treatment of Black and Asian victims. She described the scheme as 'systemically racist and unfit for purpose'.[26] The same Home Office employees who had been responsible for the plight facing postcolonial citizens were suddenly expected to assist people whose lives they had made unliveable. Furthermore, the low pay-outs themselves did not fairly compensate for the levels of financial hardship provoked by job losses, ill health and the denial of access to welfare benefits. The 'complete lack of humanity' with which Home Office workers treated claimants suggest the systemic problems remain.[27] We can see that the rhetorical distinction made between the 'deserving' Windrush generation and 'undeserving' Muslims has not translated into just treatment from the British state.

*Imperial amnesia: forgetting about 'race' and racism.*

Grappling with Prevent and the hostile environment as projects of racial bordering which operate to keep Britain white cannot be understood or resisted without also delving more deeply into colonial histories of 'race' and racism. However, this task is complicated by the twin forces of colonial amnesia (how we 'forget' aspects of British colonial history) and nostalgia (how we remember aspects of British colonial history). Colonial amnesia and nostalgia are central to the kinds of stories we tell ourselves about what Britain is and what it means to be British. This is why amnesia and nostalgia have been the subjects of fevered discussion precipitated in large part by the 2016 referendum on EU membership.

Satnam Virdee and Brendan McGeever have argued that Brexit was driven by nostalgia for the empire and the desire to rejuvenate Britain as a proud global power by 'taking back control' over its borders and keeping out undeserving populations.[28] While these debates are well-traversed elsewhere, this is a judicious moment to revisit the centrality of 'race' and racism in British history. It is only through a reckoning with this history that we can grasp how postcolonial citizens are made insecure through counter-terrorism practices and immigration regimes working to keep Britain white. But these histories must first be understood as part of the global advent of European colonialism which began in earnest around the fifteenth century.

The science of 'race' was a core aspect of European colonialism, though this idea remains controversial. While racism in contemporary liberal democracies is often regarded as an individualised pathology or a matter of persons with biases who behave in a discriminatory fashion, the history of race-making as a means through which European powers enslaved and occupied colonised people tells a rather different story. The inability of Western liberal democracies to recognise the historical and structural aspects of racial violence is tied to the rise and persistence of social movements like Black Lives Matter (BLM). BLM activists and supporters draw attention to the long-standing, wide-ranging and cyclical nature of the struggles faced by Black, Indigenous and other people of colour in the United States and elsewhere including Britain. This is because, as Alana Lentin points out, processes of race-making were central to the formation of European empires and their white settler colony offspring:

> the race concept is born of the possibilities opened up by Enlightenment methodologies; most importantly the capacity to order and classify, to rationalize everything from immaterial objects to plants, animals and human beings themselves [...] Race develops into a fully evolved system for the hierarchical ranking of humanity, from superior white to inferior black, over a long period of 200 years. This process, which leads finally to the 'Golden Age of Racism' of the late nineteenth century, is an emphatically political one.[29]

'Race' and racism not only helped divide up the world for conquest by European empires but also simultaneously cemented ideas of white superiority, authority and entitlement. Hamid Dabashi argues that Frantz Fanon's injunction that 'Europe is literally the creation of the Third World' does not simply refer to the theft of raw materials or transfers of wealth which powered European 'development' and impoverished the Global South.[30] It also refers to the very possibility of 'Europe' imagined as a civilised and civilising force presiding over an array of racialised others located elsewhere.

Through the processes of colonisation, European empires came to decide on who did and did not count as human, who could and could not be civilised. Through regimes of racial classification, colonising powers were able to turn humans into property to be traded for slavery, to dispossess indigenous people of their land on the basis that they were too 'savage' to cultivate it, and to perpetrate genocide. While there was substantial variation between and within European empires, what brought together particularistic practices of empire-craft was a shared commitment to ideas of white superiority, authority and entitlement. Whether upholding what cheerleader of British imperialism Rudyard Kipling called the 'white man's burden' or undertaking a *mission civili-satrice* to bring Christianity to indigenous peoples, the science of race provided an inexhaustible supply of knowledge that could be used by Europeans to remake and dominate the world.

David Theo Goldberg contends that these understandings of 'race' and racism have been excised from Europe through what he terms as 'political racelessness'.[31] The history of Europe is often told as the history of the European Union: a narrative of ever closer integration understood as a wholly 'internal' process without reference to or recognition of the histories of colonialism to which racialized notions of 'Europe' and the accumulation of European wealth were indebted. Goldberg argues that political 'racelessness' is embodied in the treatment of the Holocaust as 'the referent point for "race" in Europe'.[32] In particular, Goldberg argues that delinking the Holocaust from a wider global pattern of European colonialism has contributed to the erasure of histories of colonialism.

The genocidal violence of Nazi death camps was deemed internal to Europe, and has been seen as rooted in European soil. But, as the Martiniquan thinker and political activist Aimé Césaire argues, Nazism was a 'boomerang effect' of practices of racial violence already happening in European colonies across the world.[33] The historian Isabel Hull notes that the Imperial German army had engaged in acts of internment and genocide in Southwest Africa (modern day Namibia) against the Herero and Nama tribes.[34] This is where what Elizabeth Baer calls the 'genocidal gaze' was honed, premised on the dehumanisation of African populations. For Baer this logic was later replicated in the Nazi holocaust and extended to the devastation of Europe's Jewish populations.[35] As Goldberg summarises,

Colonialism [...] is considered to have taken place elsewhere, outside of Europe, and so is thought to be the history properly speaking not of Europe. Colonialism, on this view, has had little or no effect in the making of Europe itself, or of European nation-states. And its targets were solely the indigenous far removed from European soil.[36]

This reasoning leads Goldberg to conclude that there can be no thoroughgoing account of how 'race' and racism continues to structure the EU's responses to the so-called 'refugee crisis' or its border policies in the Mediterranean and North Africa. For Gurminder Bhambra, the 'refugee crisis' is in fact a crisis *of Europe* rather than a crisis *in Europe*.[37] The European context teaches us that the silencing of colonial history and its racism(s) is sustained through temporal (it happened in the past) and spatial (it happened elsewhere) dimensions. These silences also serve to obscure how the fates of people from formerly colonised spaces, whether they are already citizens of European states or attempting to attain this status, are entwined through border regimes located both outside and inside Europe. Furthermore, the refusal to acknowledge the continued power of colonial legacies in the operations of the EU obstructs debates about responsibility, reparation and justice for historic and ongoing racial violence committed in the name of Europe and its borders.

The erasure of colonial histories and their indebtedness to racism is also relevant in the British context. Historians Alan Lester, Katie Boehme and Peter Mitchell have argued that the British Empire is often construed as 'a better empire than all the others' because it was seen by those governing it (and later by those studying it), to be rooted in ideas of freedom, civilisation and liberalism.[38] To this end, it was seen as 'preferable to the alternatives at a time of rampant European imperialism' because it was an all-together 'less vicious empire than all the others'.[39] While many European empires unabashedly invoked race science in justifying their imperial pursuits, in Britain ideas of 'moderation' served to conceal the depth of racial violence both 'epistemic and physical' animating its brand of colonialism.

In other words, despite the fact that 'racial distinction and violence' were central to British imperial rule, there has been an enduring self-understanding of Britain's as 'a uniquely liberal empire' bringing the benefits of free trade and education to colonised populations so they could enjoin in the benefits of civilisation.[40] Justifications for colonialism which were premised on ideas of freedom, civilisation and liberalism mediated and concealed the racial violence that drove the British Empire. The disappearance of 'race' is also reflected in the historiography of the British Empire, which has been divided as to the extent to which racism underpinned its colonial exploits. Historian Bill Schwarz has noted that there is 'a certain discomfort about confronting questions of race' with some historians describing the British Empire as 'accidental', 'benign' and even 'beneficent'.[41]

It is unsurprising, therefore, that parts of the British public consistently demonstrate feelings of 'pride' in its colonial history despite the absence of public and formal education about the British Empire. Triumphant narratives have been echoed by successive Prime Ministers including Liz Truss, Boris Johnson, David Cameron, Gordon Brown and Tony Blair who have all at some difficult point in their leadership called for celebrations of the British Empire. Furthermore, in recent years we have seen the revival of ideas about the swashbuckling ingenuity of the British Empire from public historians like Niall Ferguson. Alongside this there have also been calls to resuscitate not just the reputation of the British Empire but also aspects of colonial practice as 'possible ethical resources for contemporary deployment'.[42]

We can see that while the history of the British Empire is not taught in schools, a self-serving narrative about it is nostalgically commemorated in public life and popular culture. Georgie Wemyss calls this narrative the 'Invisible Empire' which 'consistently asserts particular narratives of Britain's past while suppressing alternative histories [...] and histories of white violence. When it does acknowledge the British Empire, it is a discourse of merchants and the spread of civilization that suffocates competing memories.'[43]

These commemorations and erasures which they rely on add up to 'histories that work to legitimise the dominant group, whilst marginalising subordinate groups' claims to share local or national space'.[44] In sum, colonial amnesia generates an understanding of 'Britishness' as a whiteness which excludes postcolonial citizens and their ancestors from being integral to the formation of Britain's past, its present, and its future.

## 'New Beginnings': from Empire to nation

At the end of the Second World War, Britain was coming to terms with the reality of decolonisation or the gradual and often deeply violent loss of much (but not all) of its empire. For Barnor Hesse and Salman Sayyid this period reconfigured rather than dismantled 'historic relations of dependency and subordination'.[45] Moreover, decolonisation was accompanied by what Hesse and Sayyid call The Great Unknowing, 'a collective amnesia about, and systematic disavowal of, "empire"' which was 'interpreted as a new beginning'.[46] The shift from empire to nation and the amnesia which came with it was vital in shaping the contours of 'Britishness' as whiteness. Decolonisation did not just bring about the loss of colonial possessions – a process that is often noted as having been 'completed' in the 1960s – but also saw the arrival of Black and brown subjects to Britain. Their presence threw into sharp relief the dormant racist hierarchy of belonging which underpinned the British Empire and determined who counted as 'British' and who did not.

Paul Gilroy's seminal work *There Ain't no Black in the Union Jack* showed how 'Britishness' as whiteness is the product of colonial histories which continue to shape ideas of belonging and exclusion in Britain.[47] Notions of white superiority, authority and entitlement were honed in the white settler colonies of Australia, South Africa, New Zealand and Rhodesia (now Zimbabwe). Schwarz shows how these frontiers located far from the metropolitan centre of Britain came to serve as vanguards of whiteness because of their very position at the edge of the empire.[48] The relationship between Britain and white settler colonies enabled 'the codification of ideas of racial hierarchies'.[49] In their work of violently domesticating indigenous populations and creating havens of extraction, these white settler colonies were important in transmitting some of the key ways whiteness came to be meaningful in the British metropole.

Not only did colonists believe they were imbued with qualities of white superiority, but they were vocal about the perpetual danger of being usurped by the racialized colonial over whom they ruled.[50] Another important aspect of white settlers' racial ideas was the supposed threat posed by 'metropolitan politicians' located in Britain. The liberal homilies of these politicians to a unified empire in which all subjects were supposedly equal was regarded as a betrayal of the work that white settlers were undertaking.[51] Settlers viewed themselves as having authentic knowledge of colonised others and an everyday understanding of the threats the latter posed to white order. Crucially for our discussion these histories and their investments in white superiority, authority and entitlement were revived and put to work in the very different context of British post-war decolonisation. Schwarz argues that whiteness in the British metropole was 'understated', reflecting dominant liberal rhetoric about British subjects with equal rights.[52] This was in comparison to the more masculine and explicit forms that whiteness took on in Australia or Canada in the service of settler colonialism.[53] However, the process of decolonisation and the attendant loss of imperial possessions and arrival of colonial subjects nevertheless unleashed waves of racial anxiety within the British metropole.

Camilla Schofield has shown how the continued violent struggle of white settler colonies in Australia, South Africa and Rhodesia to maintain an explicit racial apartheid during this period fed into the broader racial fears precipitated by decolonisation in Britain.[54] Therefore, the tripartite fears of the loss of white authority, the usurpation by threatening racial others, and a betrayal at the hands of out-of-touch politicians, combined to fundamentally shape the debates on belonging in postcolonial Britain. These themes were also mediated through the peculiar context of the end of the Second World War. A powerful idea emerged about white Britons who had sacrificed so much during the war and were now being asked to accept the arrival of Black and brown citizens and share national resources they felt rightly belonged to them.[55] Immigration was seen as a betrayal and this view was best encapsulated by one politician who came to act as a lightning rod for white discontent.

Enoch Powell's notorious 1968 'Rivers of Blood' speech embodied racial anxieties which centred on 'the black man having the whip hand over the white man', reproducing settler colonial fears of racial usurpation.[56] Powell argued that Britain was undergoing a 'total transformation' due to the arrival of 'Commonwealth immigrants and their descendants' through which good English folk 'found themselves made strangers in their own country'.[57] Furthermore, for Powell 'The West Indian or Indian does not, by being born in England, become an Englishman. In law he becomes a United Kingdom citizen by birth; in fact he is still West Indian or Asian'.[58] He railed against the immigration policies of the incumbent Conservative government arguing they were a betrayal of white Britons who had suffered much in the war and made the case for the repatriation of postcolonial citizens.

Schofield argues that Powell was an ardent defender of Britain as a white nation which needed to shake off its obligations to Commonwealth states for a 'clean break' with its colonial past.[59] However, as Schofield's work reminds us, readings of Powell which are shorn of the broader context of British imperial rule in which he was steeped limit how we can think of the racial continuities between empire and nation. Powell, who had youthful aspirations of becoming the Viceroy of India, lamented upon its independence from British rule in 1947 that 'one's world has altered'.[60] A whole generation of the British political class who had been raised on a diet of empire was confronted with its sudden collapse. Those who had been instructed into ideas about their entitlements, the kind of lives they would lead and what those lives would mean watched as these centuries-old certainties imploded in a matter of mere decades.

Gilroy argues that, as a consequence, this history of empire 'became a source of discomfort, shame and perplexity' best embodied by Powell and his supporters.[61] This has led to what Gilroy calls a condition of 'postcolonial melancholia' characterised by the refusal to acknowledge the traumatic loss of empire and changes to Britain's national identity.[62] From this perspective we can come to understand the shift from empire to nation as one rooted in a toxic cocktail of shame, fear and denial where reinvigorated attachments to a white racial identity in the face of 'betrayal' became increasingly prominent in binding together a shell-shocked postcolonial Britain. This reality is reflected in the representation and treatment of postcolonial citizens who arrived in Britain during the period of decolonisation and since.

British Pathé newsreels from this period offer real-time glimpses into the racial anxieties of this time and how white Britons felt threatened by the arrival of their postcolonial cousins. The tensions posed by their arrival is illuminated in a short video from 1955, *Our Jamaican Problem*, in which the narrator recognises the right of West Indian immigrants to settle in Britain as equal citizens.[63] Not only did white Britons regard their jobs to be under threat from new arrivals, they also feared being undercut for wages by West Indian workers. The video also includes an interview with the Mayor of Lambeth, Councillor White, who is petitioning for controlled immigration in light of a housing crisis in the borough.

A later video from 1959, *Racial Troubles in Notting Hill*, contains an interview with Bill Symon Jordan, a member of the far-right group the White Defence League (WDL).[64] The interview is conducted in the aftermath of the Notting Hill Riots in 1958 which saw predominantly young white men targeting areas of West London in order to beat up West Indian residents. When asked if the opening of the WDL office in Notting Hill is provocative, Jordan responds by arguing that it will provide white residents with a 'constitutional' and 'political' outlet for their understandable racial frustrations. He goes on to voice fears about 'the evils of the coloured invasion' and racial 'interbreeding' which would lead to a 'mulatto' Britain and the collapse of white civilisation.

What unites both the mainstream Mayor of Lambeth and the WDL? It is the idea that Britain as a white nation will always be threatened by the presence of Black and brown citizens hailing from the Commonwealth. While the Mayor of Lambeth focused his concerns on questions of housing, the WDL were more concerned with the collapse of white British culture. These arguments are two sides of the same coin; they are expressions of white racial anxiety over who should be a citizen of white Britain and, from amongst these citizens, who should have more or less entitlement to the benefits of citizenship.

It is also clear that there is a continuity between the past and present with regards to claims made in support of 'controlled' immigration and repatriation on the basis of numbers, the supposed pressure on social infrastructure and the suppression of wages. These arguments, which are wielded today, were already being mobilised at the very onset of post-war Commonwealth immigration. These continuities reveal that for many white Britons any amount of non-white immigration has always been too much. The use of numbers became a way of making concrete an essentially unquantifiable white racial anxiety. While terms like 'invasion', 'swarms' and 'hordes' are routinely used in popular anti-immigration parlance, the fear of white replacement, once the remit of the far-right, has since been mainstreamed through academic scholarship.[65]

To unequivocally underline the connections between colonial history, white racial anxiety and the present we can also consider the phrase: 'legitimate concerns'. This is a term popularised by journalists and politicians to describe the fears of white Britons about immigration. 'Legitimate concerns' reflects an understanding that the entitlements of white Britons to the benefits of citizenship such as employment and housing should take precedence over those of postcolonial citizens. White Britons are tacitly regarded as authentic members of the nation or what far-right groups often describe as 'indigenous', who are being usurped by the less deserving Black and brown citizens.

During the 2016 referendum on British membership to the EU, the term 'London Metropolitan Elite' was used to describe politicians and voters campaigning to remain in Europe. Remain voters were described as being dismissive of leave voters who wanted to leave the EU on the basis of their 'legitimate concerns' about immigration. This framing of immigration and the tension between remainers and leavers echoes the white racial anxiety which has been felt since the period of decolonisation. The perceived betrayal of white voters by their political elite over the arrival of postcolonial citizens was at that time channelled by Powell and amplified by his supporters.

The very same feelings of betrayal have echoed down the generations and could be heard in Vote Leave's campaign during the referendum on EU membership. This time it was the feckless EU facilitating the entry of undeserving immigrants and compounding feelings of being 'left behind' among the white Britons who since 2019 have been recast as 'red wall' voters. In sum, the birth of Britain as a postcolonial nation was steeped in the shroud of white victimhood rather than the racial superiority which characterised colonial expansion. Its founding myth: the idea of little Englanders valiantly holding back the unceasing movement of racialized others from undesirable parts of the new Commonwealth to the pristine English countryside.

From this perspective, 'Britishness' can be understood as the continuous attempt to keep Britain white by settling on a national identity that marks postcolonial citizens out as interlopers and forestalls their attempts to stake a claim in the nation. From the very beginning this idea of white Britain has been driven by white anxiety and has inevitably been riven with contradictions and tensions. In Powell's view, keeping Britain white required an unceasing Burkean style vigilance against the assorted enemies of the new nation. They would be found first and foremost among Britain's postcolonial citizens.

### Britain's everyday racial borders: Prevent and the hostile environment

Racial violence at the hands of the state and society has always been a reality for Britain's Black and brown citizens. Whether this has been in relation to immigration regimes, police brutality, the criminal justice system, the existence of informal colour bars in workplaces or in terms of educational markers and health outcomes. *The Violence of Britishness* looks at how immigration rules and counter-terrorism policies work together to produce the borders of white Britain today. The book argues that the 'Prevent strategy' marked an important step in the process of entrenching the white nation further into the everyday lives of postcolonial citizens. Prevent anticipated the emergence of the hostile environment as a form of everyday racial bordering by promoting ideas of 'Britishness' which determine whether Muslims are sufficiently

British. While 'Britishness' was initially wielded to domesticate 'suspicious' Muslims it inevitably came to affect postcolonial citizens more broadly.

Formally launched in 2006, the Prevent strategy was intended to pre-emptively address the threat of radicalisation before terrorist violence could take place. However, Prevent has never simply been an exercise in pre-emptive violence prevention but is fundamentally concerned with the more complicated and colonially inflected task of domesticating Muslims to the white British nation. Domestication, according to Ghassan Hage, is a colonially inflected practice of nation building which subjugates those considered to be 'others' inside a national home where some belong and others do not.[66] Hage argues that, historically, the work of domestication functioned to incorporate working class populations and women, but also nature, animals and plant life into the service of the nation understood as a home.[67]

In the aftermath of 7/7, Muslims in Britain found themselves being assigned collective responsibility for acts of violence committed by a minority of co-religionists. Prevent was issued as an invitation to the 'Muslim community' to reform itself – understood as a racialised homogenous mass, which was threatening to, and outside of, Britishness. Muslims have since been compelled to participate in Prevent-based reforms – forms of domestication – in order to make themselves more 'British'. They have been invited to demonstrate their Britishness through practices of everyday racial bordering, where the failure to do so brings with it the risk of being designated as extremist and liable to state intervention.

The so-called 'hostile environment' replicates these logics of racial bordering, which compel postcolonial citizens to demonstrate their Britishness. However, this time it is not for the purpose of domestication that serves the national home, but in order to determine whether people have the right to access public goods and services. The hostile environment has overseen the expansion of immigration checks for those seeking to access the NHS, welfare support, educational provisions, housing, banking services and employment.[68] Though the hostile environment was a policy ostensibly aimed at making life more difficult for non-citizens and encouraging them to 'self-deport', the Windrush scandal showed that Britain's postcolonial citizens are also subject to its violence. This is because postcolonial citizens are not seen as being unconditionally British – because they are not white. As Eric Pickles, the minister for communities and local government, warned at the time, 'anyone foreign looking' could get caught up in the hostile environment.[69] While racist immigration policies have been a fixed feature of Britain's post-war settlement, it is the everyday quality of racialised borders which marks this phase as particularly pernicious.

Once upon a time, globalisation theory foretold tales of a 'borderless world'.[70] But scholars have instead noted the increasing centrality of borders in global, regional and domestic political contexts. Étienne Balibar for instance suggests that borders have become deterritorialised or delinked from the geography of the state, with border checks increasingly taking place outside of the state.[71] Furthermore, borders have proliferated within states to become part of the fabric of *everyday life*. Nira Yuval-Davis and her co-authors argue for a shift in how we analyse the borders and their relevance in political and social life.[72] Whereas postcolonial citizens coming to Britain in the post-war period faced border checks at the docks or airports, they now face the border in workplaces, hospitals or universities. Yuval-Davis et al. make the case for examining 'bordering processes', or the practice of creating and policing borders, which happens at different levels.[73] Bordering processes are tied to projects of national belonging – of marking out who is included and who is not – as well as the ability to govern these very populations.[74]

Finally, this book will conclude by suggesting that in the context of ongoing crises in British politics relating to the cost of living crisis, austerity and Brexit, practices of racial bordering are more important than ever. These are what Gargi Bhattacharyya calls 'times of scarcity and survival' where there is less to go around because of the theft of public wealth into private hands through austerity and more recently the crisis capitalism of the pandemic response.[75] In 2020, while the government was refusing to extend free school meals to feed hungry children, it was also awarding to its supporters contracts for the provision of PPE worth

£3.7 billion pounds, which have been investigated by the anti-corruption organisation Transparency International as raising 'one or more red flags for corruption'.[76] Before being pressured into introducing a windfall tax on energy companies to help a citizenry struggling with steeply rising energy bills and inflation, the government response to the cost of living crisis has been that people need to work more and get better jobs.[77]

It is no coincidence that in 2022, when Britons were being forced to choose between eating and heating, the Home Office wanted to deport asylum seekers (including children) to Rwanda. In times of serious privation enacted by government policy, the spectacle of punishing the most vulnerable who come to Britain in the hope of better days has become an important aspect of governing. But this intensification of racial borders is in fact a symptom of deep political failure, when being a white Briton does not promise the same benefits it once did. David Roediger calls this the 'wages of whiteness' which refers to the material, public and psychological ways in which those racialised as white benefit from their identity.[78] This idea has long been a source of inquiry for Black scholars in the US such as W. E. B. Du Bois[79] or Cheryl Harris, whom Roediger draws on.[80] While Brexit promised a glorious restoration of sovereignty and the return of so-called 'left behind' white Britons, the payoff for many voters has been meagre indeed.

This is what John Narayan calls 'the wages of whiteness in the absence of wages', or the reactionary demand to restore the entitlements of white citizens in the face of deepening inequality and decline capturing larger sections of society.[81] Determining who is sufficiently 'British' is a means of deciding who should have the rights and entitlements of citizenship. In casting out those who are deemed inadequately 'British' and those who threaten the primacy and privileges of white Britons in times of scarcity, a return to better days is made conceivable. While the violence of Britishness has lately been meted out by home secretaries who are also people of colour, this does not disrupt the white nationalist logics underpinning the policies they enact. 'Britishness' as whiteness is the lifeboat to which ideas of national renewal have become moored. This book underlines how conceiving of 'Britishness' as racist postcolonial violence opens up new avenues for understanding how the different practices which govern, monitor and exclude postcolonial citizens and non-citizens intersect with each other.

### MPs of colour and the violence of Britishness

How can we square the idea that on the one hand, British politics is profoundly shaped by ideas of white nationalism, and on the other that Rishi Sunak is the prime minister? Or that the last three home secretaries have all been postcolonial citizens, whose experience this book is interested in charting? Some have pointed to the instrumentalization of MPs of colour being given the job of home secretary to enact immigration policies which are most likely to impact on other people of colour. As defenders of immigration policies argue, how can it be racist to control borders, when that violence is being perpetrated by people whose parents immigrated to Britain?[82]

Maya Goodfellow has noted that this is 'an effective strategy' because 'it gives a veneer of respectability' to racist policies and reinforces the idea that 'Britain will welcome you, if you "integrate", work hard and embrace being "British"'.[83] It's not just criticism of immigration policy that can be shut down, but also criticism of the individuals who enact them on the grounds that such criticism is racist.[84] When the Labour MP Florence Eshalomi asked Priti Patel if she recognised whether 'structural inequality, discrimination and racism in our country' were a problem in Britain, Patel responded by talking about her own experience of racism and said she would not take lectures from the opposition on this issue.[85]

While there is no doubt that people of colour, and women of colour in particular are subject to racial and gendered abuse in public life, particularly online, the question of whose experience of abuse counts, and whose does not is a decidedly political one. Diane Abbott, Britain's first Black woman MP, who receives nearly half of all the abusive tweets sent to female MPs in the UK, is rarely the subject of impassioned defences that are extended to Patel, Braverman and a host of white women MPs in the ranks of the Labour party. However, the presence of postcolonial citizens who are the forefront of the Conservative government, cannot be dismissed solely as a tactic for nullifying criticism of immigration policies.

The personal wealth of some MPs of colour has been flagged as a precondition on which their success is premised. While the exact assets and earnings of the rich are not always easy to pin down, Rishi Sunak's personal wealth reportedly stands at around £200 million,[86] Nadhim Zahawi's at £100 million,[87] while Sajid Javid is reportedly worth around £6 million[88] and Priti Patel reportedly just over £2 million.[89] While there is no doubt that some came from affluent backgrounds, such as Sunak, others were from more modest families including Sajid Javid and Suella Braverman. In many respects, the story of Braverman or Javid can be seen in a way that confirms deeply held conservative values, that with a bit of hard work anyone can succeed in Britain.

As Ilyas Nagdee and Azfar Shafi note, entrepreneurialism and wealth are key to understanding how some Black and brown citizens have been courted by the Conservative Party and become part of its long tradition. Therefore, Sunak is not so much a representative of his 'community' but rather a servant of 'capital' – the wealth that is the precondition for his success as a Tory MP.[90] Crucially, the success and mobility of a handful of MPs of colour in the Conservative government does not overturn the systemic challenges faced by Britain's postcolonial citizens. Many of these MPs have enacted policies that have made life harder for Black and brown people, whether this is in relation to spending cuts which disproportionately impact on people of colour or immigration policies that make deportation or family reunification harder. Their personal stories of success rely on buying into and extending the violence of Britishness – rather than making this visible or contesting it.

We can see this in the fate of Conservative MPs of colour who challenge prevailing ideological mores, like Nusrat Ghani, who lost her ministerial position in part due to her 'Muslimness'.[91] Or consider Sayeeda Warsi, who has unsuccessfully campaigned for an investigation into Islamophobia in the Conservative Party, comparing her experience to being 'in an abusive relationship' and adding 'It's not healthy for me to be there any more with the Conservative party'.[92] The realities of the violence of Britishness are that postcolonial citizens do not have to be 'ideal victims' – they might vote for the political parties that enact racist policies, they may have voted for Brexit or they might just want to keep out of politics and focus on 'getting on'. In reality, postcolonial citizens are hugely diverse in their outlook, hailing from different communities, with different values, varying levels of income and education. But the point is that the white nationalism which permeates British politics, profoundly shapes the hopes, possibilities and material realities of post-colonial citizens. Whether people accept this as a reality, whether they buy into the idea or deny it, whether they work against this or actively extend the violence of Britishness, is then, another question.

## Structure

*Chapter One* begins with the London bombings in July 2005 and the way these events were framed as a failure of the 'Muslim community' to adequately govern itself. Prevent was issued as an invitation to Muslims: accept collective responsibility for acts of individual violence and take measures to enact reform or face the disciplinary consequences. This chapter details how, through this invitation, Muslims were racialised as a homogenous mass, intrinsically threatening to and outside of 'British-ness'. Characterisations of Muslim difference through Prevent should be understood not solely as religious but as rooted in a concurrent British history of racism and colonialism. Muslims are racialised through a mixture of strategies that draw on ideas about religious, cultural, and biological differences which converge to produce an idea of 'Muslim-ness'. This understanding of Muslim difference is supplemented by a strong imaginary about the radical otherness of so-called 'Muslim' prac-tices. Prevent is fundamentally concerned with the governing of those who exhibit signs of 'Muslimness'.

*Chapter Two* deals with the ways in which Prevent has functioned to domesticate Britain's Muslim populations. Practices of domestication can be divided into three distinct but reinforcing categories: the peda-gogical, the regulatory, and the disciplinary. The pedagogical refers to how Prevent has been in the business of teaching Muslims how to interpret and practise their faith in a way that does not conflict with being good British citizens. Pedagogy has been at the heart of Prevent: from the production of citizenship material for Muslim children to establishment of study circles and the funding of Muslim organisations to promote 'moderate' understandings of Islam. The chapter then moves on to discuss the regulatory aspects of Prevent or the ways in which the management of Muslim populations has occurred through institutional and bureaucratic means. This section focuses on the transformations that have occurred within Britain's mosques and their co-option into the third sector as registered charities. This has enabled the subjection of mosques to external standards of regulation, monitoring and intervention overseen by the Charity Commission. The training of imams 'fit for Twenty-first Century Britain' has been a core concern guiding the regulation of mosques.

The final section of this chapter will move onto the more explicitly disciplinary aspects of pre-emptive counter-terrorism exemplified in the Prevent Duty (PD). The PD 'places a duty on certain bodies [...] in the exercise of their functions, to have "due regard to the need to prevent people from being drawn into terrorism".'[93] The PD effectively introduces the everyday bordering of Muslim citizens across a range of state institutions. This legislation requires workers in public sector institutions such as schools, colleges and hospitals to monitor and report individuals who may be 'vulnerable' to radicalisation. This section lays out how the PD has entrenched the racialised bordering, monitoring and management of Muslim populations.

*Chapter Three* draws together insights regarding the everyday racial bordering through Prevent to examine how the citizenship of Muslim populations is being made conditional. Many of the debates surrounding citizenship and counter-terrorism are dominated by practices of citizenship deprivation and deportation. Instead, this chapter focuses on effects of everyday racial bordering of Muslim citizens which foregrounds the possibility of citizenship deprivation. This conditionality of citizenship is reflected in how expressions of Muslimness are mobilised to contest the rights of Muslim citizens to 'act politically' or fully exercise their freedoms. This idea is explored further by looking at the gendered impacts of conditional citizenship on Muslim women and their ability to participate in public life. The chapter concludes by exploring how Muslim children in schools engage in practices of self-censorship to pre-empt accusations of extremism that may lead to a Prevent referral. The exercise of Muslim citizenship is premised on a casting out of those religious beliefs and practices which call into question their 'Britishness'.

*Chapter Four* moves us along to the 'hostile environment' policy and how these policies replicate and extend the logics of Prevent and everyday bordering targeting populations racialised as insufficiently British. In 2012, then Home Secretary Theresa May stated she wanted to 'create here in Britain a really hostile environment for illegal migration.'[94] Under the Conservative-led coalition government the Hostile Environment Working Group oversaw the introduction of immigration controls embedded within public service provision (the NHS, schools, colleges, universities, welfare benefits) and access to housing, banking, and employment. This was to deter non-citizens from settling in Britain and compelling them to leave 'voluntarily' by having to prove their entitlement to public goods, employment and housing through paperwork. The hostile environment has made the British border a bureaucratic reality of the everyday and has recreated racialised hierarchies of citizens with differential entitlements to public goods and services. Crucially, these changes were enacted with the full participation of an entire political class which capitulated to what were historically considered to be far right demands.

*Chapter Five* brings together the analysis of Prevent and the hostile environment as common examples of everyday racial bordering which produce hierarchies of citizenship and places these in their historical context. The chapter looks at how the histories of immigration legislation which sought to restrict the movement of Black and brown citizens to Britain, were animated by two key ideas: namely differential (im) mobility and dispossession. Luke de Noronha's notion of differential (im)mobilities explores the question of 'who gets to move' in global politics as 'a racial question' in relation to the deportation of Black Britons.[95] Differential (im)mobilities provide a framework to think through how Prevent and the hostile environment similarly foreground deportation but through racial bordering create everyday forms of being 'stuck' and in 'limbo' both within and outside of Britain. Nadine El-Enany's work *Bordering Britain* provides an account of dispossession through immigration legislation that is 'a final seizure of wealth'.[96] Prevent and the hostile environment can both be regarded as tools which stop the postcolonial citizens from accessing national resources as well as exercising their rights. The chapter concludes by reflecting on how colonial amnesia as a deliberate political strategy lies at the rotten heart of racial hierarchies of citizenship in Britain today.

The *Conclusion* tentatively explores how everyday racial bordering has become an increasingly vital political tool in a crisis ridden and grossly unequal Britain. 'Britishness' is a form of postcolonial violence which promises salvation for the nation in times of crisis through the restoration of white entitlement and exclusion of racialised others. Where the wages of whiteness are no longer paying as handsomely as they used to – whether through declining wages or through inadequately funded public services – racial bordering and the ability to exclude those made into undeserving citizens is more powerful than ever.

Since 2010, there have been cuts of up to 49% to local government spending in England, and government spending on public services, as a share of GDP, has been reduced from 47% to 40%.[97] This has led to crises in the provision of public goods such as welfare benefits, education, health, and social care, as well as the suppression of wages in the public sector. Against this background the Referendum on British Membership of the EU was held and 51.9% of the voting electorate voted to leave. This success was underwritten by fears about immigrants new or settled 'stealing' increasingly scarce resources from white Britons. The Covid-19 pandemic and resulting pressures on the NHS and Brexit-related shortages of labour in key sectors like social care, have compounded these pressures and a sense of building crisis. As Britain now heads into another phase of austerity, the conclusion argues that 'Britishness' functions as a form of postcolonial violence which entails a promise to rescue deserving white Britons from the machinations of the undeserving racialised poor.

# 1

# *The Invitation*

The people who brought down those towers were Muslims and Muslims must stand up and say that is not the way of Islam. Passengers on those planes were told that they were going to die and there were children on board. They must say that is disgraceful. I have not heard enough condemnation from Muslim priests.

Margaret Thatcher[1]

Muslims themselves are aware of the risk of radicalisation within certain offshoots of their communities and we must work in partnership with communities to identify and respond to the risk that extremism poses.

HM's Government[2]

While the more fanatical of the Musalmans have thus engaged in overt sedition, the whole Muhammadan community has been openly deliberating on their obligations to rebel.

William Wilson Hunter[3]

The London bombings in July 2005 marked an important moment in the relationship between the British state and its Muslim citizens. The shock of how four young men, Mohammed Sidique Khan, Shehzad Tanweer, Germaine Lindsay and Hasib Hussain, had come to perpetrate suicide bombings in London reverberated across the political establishment. Why would they, as individuals who'd received the advantages of an education, employment and established lives, commit acts of mass murder against their own fellow citizens? This framing echoed the words of US President George Bush, who, following the attacks of 9/11, posed the question, 'why do they hate us?'

The conundrum of so-called 'home grown' terrorists was deemed to be a particularly disturbing phenomenon for intelligence services. The 7/7 bombers were initially described as 'clean skins', or individuals who had prior to their crimes done nothing to attract attention. However, later it emerged that prior to the bombings MI5 did have foreknowledge of some of the activities of both Khan and Tanweer.[4] The statements of the perpetrators, in which they railed against the War on Terror and British foreign policy, did not feature in the motives attributed to the bombers by policymakers and the British press. Making sense of the bombings through critiques of Western states and their foreign policies was regarded as either morally objectionable or inadequate in its explanatory power. Blaming 'the West' or grounding analysis in anything other than the pathologized terrain of 'Islam' and 'Muslims' quickly became taboo.

Rather, the explanation for home grown terrorism was attributed to the process of 'radicalisation', whereby 'radicalised individuals [who] are using a distorted and unrepresentative version of the Islamic faith to justify violence.'[5] As part of the Prevent strategy launched in the aftermath of the bombings, it was stated that the number of 'Islamist terrorists' constituted a 'small minority' and that 'Muslim communities themselves do not threaten our security' and the government would work 'in partnership with Muslim communities to help them prevent extremists gaining influence there.'[6] The demands for Muslims to condemn terrorist violence as a way of demonstrating national loyalty were fully established after 9/11. As the epigraphs above amply demonstrate, Muslim communities were invited to accept responsibility for the violence committed by their co-religionists and were charged with the responsibility of preventing such things from happening again.

This chapter begins by looking at how 7/7 was framed as a failure of the Muslim community to govern itself. This provides essential context to looking more closely at how the Prevent strategy and its articulation of radicalisation is premised on making Britain's Muslims collectively responsible for violence carried out by those unconnected to them. The invitation to accept collective responsibility, which could not be refused, was central to making the 'Muslim community' a site of Prevent-based interventions to govern, reform and discipline British Muslims through community partnerships. The chapter then moves on to explore the British colonial and military histories of collective responsibility and their racial character. The idea of a Muslim conspiracy to overthrow British imperial power, which took root after the Indian Uprising in 1857, is particularly relevant to this discussion. Finally, returning to the present we can observe that the collective responsibility embodied in Prevent is both premised on and enabled the racialisation of Britain's Muslims as a homogenous mass threatening to white Britain.

### Terrorism as a failure of the 'Muslim community'

In the aftermath of the 7/7 bombings, the fact that the perpetrators were deemed to be 'home grown' caused particular consternation. The bombers were seen as having enjoyed all the trappings of life in the West, which would not have been afforded to them in their ancestral homelands of Pakistan and Jamaica. A report by the European Monitoring Centre for Racism and Xenophobia argued 'themes of betrayal and ingratitude towards the host society were evident in relation to two further suspects of the bombings'.[7] The most common way of making sense of the attacks was by reference to the identity of the bombers as Muslim men from Pakistani immigrant communities. Very little attention has been paid to Lindsay as the only Black and non-Pakistani perpetrator born in Jamaica, whose wife Sherafiyah Samantha Lewthwaite was infamously dubbed the 'white widow'. Instead, it was Beeston – the hometown of Khan, Tanweer and Hussain – which became the subject of journalistic voyeurism, as the search for answers landed squarely within the mysterious otherness of its residents.

Journalist Shiv Malik argued the violence was a result of 'a conflict between tradition and individuality, culture and religion, tribalism and universalism, passivity and action'.[8] He paints a picture of a community mired in the 'strict and unforgiving' structures of the Mirpuri society from which many of Beeston's Pakistani migrants came.[9] The culture clashes between community elders and second and third-generation youngsters on a range of issues such as the freedom to marry were regarded as the primary source of radicalisation. This narrative conveniently removes the bombers from wider British society and renders them a product of a self-contained or 'ghettoised' and dysfunctional Pakistani community. Malik further argued that the suggested link between poverty and terrorism was a 'red herring' and that 'internal frictions within a traditional Pakistani community' were the cause of the trouble.[10] This is despite writing about the drug problem, which had according to residents 'dragged everything down' in the area and which was the source of antagonism between the elder and younger generations. Malik's framing of cultural pathology ignored the words of the residents, who repeatedly refer to the structural inequalities faced by British Pakistanis in Beeston including racial segregation and poverty.

Instead, radicalisation came to be understood as a symptom of the broader failure of multiculturalism which, according to British policymakers, had allowed Muslims to live segregated lives. Here, the easy slippage between speaking of 'Pakistanis' and then 'Muslims' is telling of the racial ambiguity which runs through discourses on radicalisation, where the identity of those 'at risk' of radicalisation is always confidently presumed but does not rest on solid ground. Nevertheless, the 'failure of multiculturalism' was pronounced by other European leaders including German Chancellor Angela Merkel and French President Nicolas Sarkozy; this supposed failure was particularly important in appealing to liberal sentiments about why Muslims were a 'problem' minority.

Sivamohan Valluvan has argued that liberal nationalism is premised on the idea that the 'white citizen is instilled, by default, with a civic, universalist ethos while the racialised citizen, first-generation and otherwise, acquires these qualities'.[11] This is a crucial idea for getting to grips with how different political registers of racism frame Muslim populations as a problem population appealing to different types of political constituencies spanning from the right, across the centre and the left. The notion that Muslim communities were falling short and that they needed to be made into 'literate members of the national culture' was indeed popular among the left and liberal intelligentsia who might otherwise have balked at the loss of long-cherished civil liberties in the service of the nation.[12]

For example, the 2001 summer 'riots' in the North of England provoked by the resurgent presence of far-right organisations in places such as Bradford and Oldham saw the depiction of South Asian and particularly British Pakistani men as poorly adjusted, culturally conflicted and violent. The subsequent Cantle Report into the events argued that it was racial and ethnic segregation which led to the violence, rather than the presence of the far-right in these towns.[13] Integration and social cohesion or the pursuit of a mono-cultural British national identity were the officially formulated police responses to the violence of the far-right.[14] After 9/11, the 'riots' were re-characterised as an unheeded warning about the dangers to the nation posed by British Muslims and particularly Muslim men. The answer to 'how could this happen?' lay not in the structures of racial, gendered and class inequality but in a fully pathologized 'Muslim community'.

This is reflected in the most disturbing aspect of Malik's account of how he insinuated himself into the life of Gultasab Khan, the brother of Mohammed Sidique Khan, and visited his house which sat 'at the nice end of a nice street' despite being asked not to.[15] The house itself is described as 'sparsely decorated 'and 'unnervingly clean' as though this provides necessary context into the psyche of this particular family and a wider community.[16] However, Malik saves his most pronounced voyeuristic tendencies for the wife of Gultasab, who is noted as being 'tall and dressed in a brightly coloured salwar kameez, her head uncovered'.[17] After a brief chat with Gultasab in the corridor Malik never sees her again. The entitlement which underpins Malik's desire for access to the family and the implicit sense of frustration about why this is not forthcoming is rendered as a shortcoming of the family itself. In this orientalist framing of the wife with her uncovered head, brightly adorned and hidden from view by the Muslim husband, Malik does not stop to consider that his intrusive and unwanted presence in her home might explain her absence.

Malik's account of the bombers, focused on internal community pathologies, was emblematic of the dominant way of thinking about radicalisation: as a failure of Muslim communities to govern themselves adequately by integrating into British society and in so doing keep their youth in check. Debates about the complex relationship between race, class and violence were marginalised in policy making in favour of a simplified narrative of young Muslims caught between a liberal life in Britain and the conservatism of their immigrant parents. This genera-tion were regarded as being seduced by the Manichean certainties of a 'distorted' version of Islam. 'Wahhabism', 'Islamism' and 'Salafi-Jihad-ism' all came to serve as placeholder terms for why terrorism is 'caused' by Islam. It is through this toxic mixture of pathologizing Muslim com-munities through discourses on British Pakistanis and civilisational framings of Islam that the Prevent strategy was born.

While some key Muslim organisations and prominent figures sought to draw attention to the political and socio-economic factors which may drive violence, the British Prime Minister Tony Blair placed the blame squarely within the realm of religion and the 'evil' and 'barbaric' strain of Islam bearing 'hatred of the West and our way of life'.[18] According to this view, there were 'moderate' Muslims and an extremist minority rep-resented by organisations like al-Qaeda which needed to be confronted. Blair proclaimed that 'within Britain, we must join up with our Muslims community to take on the extremists'.[19] It is this invitation to prevent radicalisation that was issued to a 'Muslim community' understood as both pathologically dysfunctional but also as collectively responsible for terrorist violence.

*Invitation to prevent? Partnerships and power*

In the 2015 horror film *The Invitation*, the protagonist, Will, reluctantly accepts an invite to a dinner party hosted by his ex-wife Eden from whom he is divorced following the death of their child.[20] His hesitancy in attending is surpassed by the desire to see Eden, with whom he shares a traumatic bond of grief but from whom he has become estranged over time. During the course of their evening it eventually comes to light that the hospitality of Eden and her new partner conceals darker motives, namely that they have joined a cult and intend to poison their guests in a suicide-murder pact. As the evening progresses and with increas-ing feelings of dread, Will comes to feel the horror lurking beneath the surface of this aggressively bourgeois dinner party. He exclaims, 'something dangerous is going on and we're all just ignoring it because David brought some good wine?!'[21]

The film provides a useful way of framing Prevent as an invitation that could not be refused by British Muslims. Prevent was framed as an opportunity for Muslim civil society to positively shape the lives of British Muslims in response to radicalisation and extremism. However, the premise of the invitation was the acceptance of collective responsibility for what had been characterised as the collective failure of terrorism. But, just as Will could not refuse the invitation to that fateful dinner party despite his unease, so Muslim civil society could not pass up an opportunity to have their specific but neglected concerns about inequality and Islamophobia addressed. In this scenario the 'good wine' was New Labour's promise to tackle anti-Muslim hate crime and the high levels of disadvantage faced by Muslims in Britain. In exchange, the government stressed the unique responsibility of Muslims at large for tackling radicalisation. Consequently, these partnerships would prove to be something of a double-edged sword for Muslim civil society: the something 'dangerous' being the very premise of partnerships enabled by Prevent.

The New Labour government had adopted the Muslim Council of Britain (MCB) as a key partner in its response to 9/11 and the War on Terror. The MCB is a Muslim umbrella organisation which was established in 1997 and represents 500 Muslim member groups including 'mosques, charities, schools and member groups.'[22] They were, in a neo-colonial fashion, considered by the New Labour government to be 'leaders' of the Muslim community. Jonathan Birt notes that the MCB was expected to deliver the support of British Muslims for the military interventions of the War on Terror in return for access to the New Labour government.[23] For instance, the MCB successfully lobbied on issues such as including the religion question on the national census to facilitate information gathering on the inequalities faced by Britain's Muslims. However, the organisation was not able to secure the support of British Muslims for the war in Iraq and, as a result, the short-lived alliance between New Labour and the MCB fell apart. The MCB was later accused by the New Labour government of having links to extremists and were 'effectively accused of having exacerbated religious separatism'.[24]

These events set the tone for the ways in which successive governments would choose to engage with those Muslim partners who were more or less sympathetic to government policy and how they would be treated. Muslim groups who exhibited anything less than full acceptance of Prevent and the War on Terror were discredited by being linked to 'Islamists' or accused of being 'terrorist apologists'. It is clear that the boundary between an 'extremist' and a 'moderate' is in part an exercise in state power which serves to uphold and extend this power and protect it from criticism. Birt writes that the government adviser Faz Hakim 'called upon Muslims to reassess their position': 'are they bringing up kids to be anti-British and anti-Jewish? They have to think'.[25] The seamless rhetorical shift from recalcitrant Muslim partners with links to extremism to individual Muslims raising their children in 'anti-British' ways exemplified how logics of collective responsibility underpin the characterisations of and engagement with British Muslims. Muslims are suspect not because of their actions but by virtue of their identity.

The unequal and strained partnership approach was reflected in the creation of the 'Preventing Extremism Together' working groups (PET). The PETs sought to analyse 'what had happened on those two days in July' and 'what motivated the four July 7 bombers'.[26] Muslim partners were engaged on issues such as education, policing and the position of Muslim women to 'tackle extremism and radicalisation'. They also drew attention to issues of 'inequality, discrimination, deprivation and inconsistent Government policy, and in particular foreign policy'.[27] However, once the New Labour government had clarified its approach to preventing violent extremism there was little focus on the structural inequalities facing Britain's Muslims. The aim of counter-radicalisation was 'winning the hearts and minds' of Muslim populations and isolating radical elements by empowering so-called 'moderate' voices'. The focus was squarely on Muslim communities to do this work of counter-radicalisation.

After the attacks of 9/11, Margaret Thatcher said in an interview with *The Times* that she had not heard enough condemnation of the attacks from Muslim 'priests'. Though Thatcher was widely condemned for her remarks at the time, including from those within her own party for conflating terrorism and religion, her words were instructive. They laid bare the logics of future counter-radicalisation programmes such as Prevent, which would effectively displace collective responsibility for terrorism onto Muslim communities and frame acts of terrorism as the failure of Muslims at large. Characterisations of the Muslim population as collectively responsible for terrorist violence, which surfaced after 9/11 and 7/7, were eventually translated into policy through the Prevent strategy.

This was despite the early attempts, in public statements by New Labour and the US government, to draw distinctions between Islam as a religion observed peaceably by millions of people and a violent radical minority. Nevertheless, the actual workings of counter-extremism programmes like Prevent exposed this rhetorical sleight of hand. Muslims were construed as a suspect community whose members were all potential radicals in waiting. This is the pre-emptive space carved out by Prevent for the prevention of 'radicalisation'. The invitation to accept collective responsibility for 7/7 was one that could not be refused, underpinned by differential power relations between the New Labour government and Muslim civil society that would ultimately lead to catastrophe for Britain's Muslims.

### Race, collective responsibility and collective punishment

In early 2020, Trevor Phillips, the former chair of the UK's Equalities and Human Rights Commission (EHRC) was suspended from the Labour Party pending further investigation for describing Muslims as a 'nation within a nation' and noting how few Muslims wore poppies on Remembrance Day.[28] Phillips stated, 'They say I am accusing Muslims of being different. Well, actually, that's true. The point is Muslims are different.'[29] He further argued that Muslims should be judged collectively: 'the truth is, if you do belong to a group, whether it is a church, or a football club, you identify with a particular set of values, and you stand for it. And frankly you are judged by that'.[30] In 2021, Phillips, now working as a host for Sky News was quietly reinstated as a member of a Labour Party that had been at the same time beset by scandals around anti-Semitism. The Labour MP for Poplar and Limehouse, Apsana Begum, said his readmission was 'without explanation or apology' and represented an 'insult to my community'.[31]

Phillips' sentiments, his fate and the response of the Labour Party are all useful indicators of how the logic of collective responsibility works in relation to Muslims. It has become a common-sense view to regard Muslims in Britain as a homogenised group. Because Muslims have 'shared values' they must all be judged for those. On this basis, liberal and conservative defenders of Phillips postulate that criticism of Muslims as adherents of Islam rather than as a 'race' must be defended on grounds of free speech.[32] 'Muslims are not a race' is something that everyone from the far-right English Defence League (EDL) to urbane liberal journalists can seem to agree on. The All Parliamentary Party Group on British Muslims definition of Islamophobia as a 'form of anti-Muslim racism' was contested on this basis. The definition was singled out by Phillips supporters as a way of closing down 'legitimate criticism' about Muslims and Islam.[33]

The fact Phillips was reinstated into the Labour Party without comment and continues to occupy a prominent place in public life where he regularly speaks on matters regarding (in)equalities and racism, underscores the everyday banality of Islamophobia. For Aditya Chakrabortty, Phillip's reinstatement signalled the Labour Party's pivot towards the Islamophobic political mainstream in Britain, which means appealing to 'traditional' (white) voters who are all assumed to be racist.[34] So, how did the British mainstream become openly Islamophobic? This is where we arrive at the crux of the matter: the relationship between 'race', collective responsibility and collective punishment. The idea of a Muslim community collectively responsible for the actions of all Muslims is at its heart a racial idea steeped in hidden British colonial anxieties and military experiences. Collective responsibility not only draws on these histories but allows for new racial possibilities to open up, new ways of meting out collective punishment. Prevent is but the latest iteration of collective responsibility narrative central to codifying Muslims as a homogenous mass that is threatening to white Britain and in need of punishment.

## The histories of collective responsibility: COIN and conspiracy

Ratified in 1959, the Geneva Conventions are at the heart of the International Law of Armed Conflict, the rules which govern how wars should be fought. The Geneva Conventions prohibited the use of collective punishment which was a direct response to the mass violence perpetrated against European civilians by warring European powers during the two world wars. While the Geneva Conventions were seen as a shift towards entrenching humanitarian safeguards in the waging of war between sovereign states, they did not initially apply to the violence enacted by European colonial powers against their colonised populations. Wars of national liberation and decolonisation struggles waged by non-state actors in colonies were invariably described as 'emergencies' and 'counter-insurgencies' (COIN). Thus, they escaped the protections offered by the Geneva Conventions to European sovereign states and their peoples.

British counter-insurgency operations in Malaya, Kenya and Cyprus, all colonies struggling for freedom from colonial rule, were characterised by the use of collective punishment against populations considered to be racially inferior. Mass torture, mass incarceration and mass killing were all features of British attempts to supress decolonial movements erupting in different parts of the empire. Military historian Brian Drohan has shown that human-rights based criticism of Britain's COIN campaigns were met with lies and evasion.[35] Kim Wagner argues that this evasion connotes a broader inability to reckon with the violence of the British Empire, which was regarded as more humane in its treatment of colonised populations than its German, Belgian and Dutch counterparts.

As Wagner writes, the wider 'racial and cultural hierarchies prevalent in the West during the second part of the nineteenth century [...] permeated military thinking and practice.'[36] The notion of 'savage warfare' rested on the view that colonised populations in Africa, Asia and the Middle East were racially inferior and did not fight like civilised Europeans. Military violence saturated with racial thinking was constitutive of the establishment of European empires and, for the British, was happening at the 'high point of Empire'.[37] Why is this relevant for how we think about collective responsibility, collective punishment and 'race'? After all, isn't Prevent a contemporary domestic counter-terrorism programme which supposedly deals with all forms of extremist threat in the UK?

For Rizwaan Sabir this is a misdiagnosis of Prevent which should be understood as akin to COIN, or population-centred conflict which encompasses 'soft' as well as 'hard' forms of power.[38] The resuscitation of COIN principles for waging the conflicts of the War on Terror in Afghanistan and Iraq have been widely explored elsewhere, but Sabir shows this thinking has made its way to the 'home front'. Crucially, it is the idea of the 'global jihad' which enabled the proliferation of COIN from so-called international theatres of conflict to domestic settings. The understanding that Muslims anywhere – whether they are found in the 'Muslim world' or in Europe or the Anglosphere – can be potentially threatening to Western power and interests has been at the heart of the War on Terror. For Sabir the emphasis on surveillance and propaganda which occurs through Prevent also characterised the low intensity colonial warfare waged through COIN.[39] Furthermore, Prevent is not premised on consent prized by liberal democracies but coercion and 'blurs' the distinction between civilians and combatants.

Thinking about COIN helps us to make sense of how Prevent has made Britain a home front in the global War on Terror. This insight returns us to how we can think about the relationship between collective responsibility, collective punishment and 'race'. Historic COIN campaigns were waged by European empires to suppress and dispel any resistance to colonial rule. COIN was premised on ideas of the racial alterity and inferiority of colonised people; they enabled the mass killing, incarceration and torture of anyone considered to be part of a problem community threatening colonial power. It is precisely this view of the collective responsibility of all Muslims for terrorism through the notion of global jihad which animates the War on Terror and Prevent.

Moreover, in Britain, ideas about the 'threatening' Muslims and the 'dangerous' religion of Islam also have a longer history than is commonly acknowledged. In 1857, when Hindu sepoys and Muslim sowars in the East India Company's Bengal Army sparked an uprising against their erstwhile rulers, a visceral sense of disbelief overcame the British in India and in the metropole. Alan Lester, Kate Boehme and Peter Mitchell argue that the uprising was more than 'a mere soldiers' mutiny' but the consequence of 'the much broader coalition' which developed against company misrule.[40] This included increasingly aggressive tax extraction, the annexation of ever greater swathes of India bought under company control and the racial contempt with which Indians were treated.[41] The uprising began in military cantonments in Meerut and spread to Delhi, Kanpur and Lucknow in the north of India, encompassing 'nobleman, clerics, artisans, local officials, minor landlords, merchants and peasants' across Northern India.[42] It lasted for more than a year, before being gradually crushed by the British who had mobilised forces from across the empire in defence of their presence in India.

British shock at the uprising lay in the moral certitude about the desirability of colonialism and the supposed benefits it brought to colonised populations. Such views which were embodied in the influential work of philosophers like John Stuart Mill, whose writings company officials studied in their formal training at Haileybury. Priyamvada Gopal has argued that the British fundamentally considered themselves a force for good, bringing technological, political and social progress to the unenlightened colonised masses.[43] Wagner also underscores how the British felt they intimately knew the land and the people they ruled over.[44] These assumptions were important in making sense of the brutal suppression of the uprising which, as Gopal notes, was marked by the killings of 'tens of thousands of Indians' often in deliberately vindictive and frenzied ways.[45] This violence was characteristic of the 'hysterical racial outrage' which marked the British response both in India and in the metropole.[46] Stories of India sepoys violating, mutilating and murdering British women and children became the focus of British outrage.

The East India Company, which had ruled since 1757, was swept away by royal decree and the age of the British Raj, an India being directly governed by the British crown, began.

One of the chief legacies of this time was the idea of a 'Mussulman conspiracy', an idea that emerged through British investigations into the causes of the uprising.[47] This view was grounded in a racialised imaginary about Muslims and the nature of Islam. Ideas of Muslim conspiracy emerged partly due to the fact that Bahadur Shah Zafar, the last Mughal emperor, was championed by many of the rebels as an alternative to company rule. At Shah's trial the presiding judge claimed that Hindu sepoys had been manipulated by their fanatical Muslim counterpoints. However, beyond being a figurehead, there was no evidence to support the idea of a concerted Muslim conspiracy led by Shah to overthrow the British. Like all conspiracy theories, the power of the Muslim conspiracy did not lie in its veracity but in the political functions it fulfilled.

Alex Padamsee has argued that ideas of Muslim fanaticism, Muslim bigotry and Muslim criminality pre-dated the 1857 Uprising.[48] These discourses enabled the 'recasting of socio-economic grievances against colonialism into the narrative of "religious prejudice"' supposedly embodied by Indians, which elicited a 'law and order' response from British authorities.[49] In other words, any threat to British rule was read as a problem of the internal characteristics and working of a particular religion, caste or group. Muslims were placed as foreign interlopers in India – a discourse replicated by Narendra Modi and the BJP in India today – and the British as the preservers of Indian society.[50] These developments ran alongside moves to create an Indian army whose upper echelons were increasingly incorporating the 'martial races' or upper caste Hindus and Sikhs. These discourses were underwritten by the understanding that 'acts performed by Muslims were, by definition, committed by Muslims *as* Muslims'.[51] This idea was the basis of the Muslim conspiracy.

After the uprising, Padamsee argues, the Muslim conspiracy was seen to rest on three primary assumptions: that 'Muslim discontent centre(s) on the dispossession of the former Mughal rulers; the natural and irresistible appeal of militant opposition to all Indian Muslims; and the

Christian identity of the British rulers as an essentialised provocation to their religious temperament'.[52] Muslims were racialised as having a predilection for violence and a bloodthirsty nature that drove their irascible jihad to overthrow the British. These views were reflected in the writings of prominent and powerful Indian Civil Servants (ICS) of the time. In 1857, ISC Alfred Lyall wrote in his personal correspondence that 'the Mahometans only seem to care about murdering their opponents, and are altogether far more bloody-minded. Those last hate us with a fanatical hate…'[53]

Later, in 1871, another ICS, William Wilson Hunter, wrote a highly influential book entitled *The Indian Musalmans: Are They Bound in Conscience to Rebel Against the Queen?* Hunter's account of disloyal Muslims states that:

The Musalmans of India are, and have been for many years, a source of chronic danger to British power in India. For some reason or other they hold aloof from our system, and the changes in which more flexible Hindus have cheerfully acquiesced are regarded by them as deep personal wrongs.[54]

According to this view, networks of Wahhabi conspirators were ready to incite a pan-Indian Muslim insurrection to bring down the British. Muslims were racialised as collectively threatening to colonial rule by virtue of their faith which the British regarded as an aggressive, vindictive and intolerant religion.

*Prevent: saving (white) Britain from Muslims*

The continuities between colonial ideas characterising Muslims as a danger to British colonial power and contemporary discourses on terrorism and extremism are striking. While there is no longer an overarching concern with the preservation of colonial rule, it is the Muslim threat to the (white) British nation which now overwhelms the political imagination. Narratives about disloyal Muslims susceptible to becoming radicalised sit alongside allusions to covert extremist Muslim forces fanning the flames of a global jihad. These ideas permeate how policymakers, security practitioners and the wider public think about radicalisation and terrorism as threats intrinsic to the very presence of Muslim populations. This final part of this chapter shows how Prevent draws on colonial logics of collective responsibility to recast Muslims as an enemy within, one seeking to supplant the white British nation. Prevent is central to the production of state-led Islamophobia because of its role in codifying the racial alterity of Muslims and Islam.

Prevent is a pre-emptive counter-radicalisation scheme to 'stop people becoming terrorists or supporting terrorism'.[55] It is designed to target all types of terrorist threats including those from the far-right. According to policymakers, the focus on 'Islamist' terrorism merely reflects the level of threat facing Britain from extremist groups in Syria, Iraq and Afghanistan. Prevent is characterised as another form of safeguarding which protects the welfare of vulnerable or at-risk children and adults. Through the Prevent Duty (explored in more detail in Chapter 3), radicalisation prevention is now a statutory obligation in the public sector for schools, colleges, universities, the NHS and Her Majesty's Prison Service.

Frontline staff are trained to spot the signs of radicalisation among their students, prisoners and patients, who may then be referred to the de-radicalisation programme: Channel. In recent years, 'far-right' Prevent referrals have been increasing and 'far-right' Channel cases now outstrip 'Islamist' cases. In fact, the rising attention being paid to the 'far-right' is used as evidence of the neutrality and adaptability of Prevent to counter accusations of racism. 'Prevent works where it is needed' is the take home message in these instances. Nonetheless, the fact remains that since its launch in 2006, Prevent has focused overwhelmingly on Muslim communities, often in profoundly racialised ways. Indeed, in a recent review of Prevent, William Shawcross, the former head of the Charity Commission with a record of making Islamophobic statements and focusing on Muslim charities, argued that the programme was too focused on the far right.[56]

The rising rates of far-right individuals espousing white nationalist views and wielding violence have not led to accusations of community failure among white Britons or community-based interventions of the kind that have been directed at Britain's Muslims. Despite the growing threat of violent attacks by white nationalists which is reflected in Prevent referrals, there is no corresponding moral panic or policy action to address this problem. Therefore, the significance of Prevent cannot be adequately understood through the numbers game of referrals alone. It is the way in which Prevent has been central to constructing and circulating ideas of Muslims as outside of and threatening to the white British nation. Prevent has propagated racialised ideas of radicalisation and extremism that casts Muslims as an existential threat and the white 'far-right' as a nuisance alongside animal rights activists and environmental campaigners.

The idea of a 'Muslim community' collectively responsible for terrorist violence was formalised through Prevent and lies at the heart of the strategy. This is despite the changes in emphasis and implementation between early Prevent (2006–11) and later Prevent (2011– the present). Early Prevent, pioneered by the New Labour government, was explicitly focused on the threat of 'Islamist' radicalisation within the 'Muslim community'. As a result, the idea of community cohesion emerged as a core plank of preventing radicalisation and extremism. Prevent delivery cut across multiple central government departments, local authorities, the police and community and charity organisations. This was reflective of New Labour's idea of a 'joined-up government', undergirded by the view that major social problems such as social exclusion or crime could not be the remit of one government department. Structural problems required a structural governmental approach.

More precisely, the designation of collective responsibility was enabled by the emergence of the idea of radicalisation as the leading cause of terrorist violence. While 'radicalisation' is not a new concept, it is one which has gained increasing purchase since 9/11. Contemporary understandings of radicalisation have their antecedents in earlier pre-9/11 analysis of the Red Army Faction in Germany and the Red Brigades in Italy. Germany and Italy were facing political crises in which their own citizens were taking up arms against them in the name of revolutionary change. At this time, research on terrorism was sometimes characterised by its focus on the psychological causes of radicalisation and the supposed prevalence of mental health disorders amongst terror-ists.[57] Contemporary explanations of radicalisation do not begin from the premise that terrorists are 'crazy'. Rather, radicalisation explains the journey of a 'vulnerable' or 'at-risk' person from being merely sus-ceptible to radical ideas to becoming someone who commits an act of political violence.

Writing in 2010, 'terrorism expert' Magnus Ranstorp argued that in the aftermath of 9/11, 'understanding violent radicalization was critical but an enigma to most experts whether in government or academia'.[58] Fortunately for Ranstorp and others like him, this gap in understand-ing became something of an intellectual goldrush: an opportunity for career advancement, research funding and media exposure in the now globally lucrative industry of Preventing Violent Extremism (PVE). Lisa Stampnitzky's account of the role of terrorism experts in determin-ing how terrorism is understood and how counter-terrorist responses are shaped, shows that the contested nature of terms like 'terrorism' is politically productive.[59] Just as terrorism experts argue that terrorism is an essentially contested concept so the same can be said for radicalisa-tion. However, the enigmatic character of these categories has opened up space for 'experts' to come forth and offer frameworks for thinking about political problems that cohere with government security agendas across the globe. This is precisely what has happened with radicalisation.

In Britain, the post 7/7 emergence of radicalisation as an explanatory framework for terrorism was exclusively concerned with the Muslims and Islam. Early Prevent characterised radicalisation as the product of 'warped thinking' which happens through 'using a distorted and unrepresentative version of Islam'.[60] This view underscored how policy-makers considered radicalisation as a problem synonymous with being Muslim. This was also a critique expressed by scholars of the 'suspect communities' thesis who argued that counter-terrorism policies have made British Muslims into a suspect community where the 'blame' for terrorism is carried by the collective.[61] As Arun Kundnani eloquently puts it, radicalisation was another way of asking 'why [do] some indi-vidual Muslims support an extremism version of Islam that leads to violence?'[62] Models of radicalisation, whether causal, complex or social were rooted in the presumptions about the religious beliefs of Muslims and their psychological condition.

The 2009 iteration of Prevent justified the overwhelming focus of counter-radicalisation practices on Muslim populations by the scale of the threat posed by 'those who claim to act in the name of Islam'.[63] The shifting focus on the far right would not happen, at least on paper, until later. In the meantime, Prevent established three principles regarding counter-radicalisation. Firstly, that radicalisation is an immanent security threat within Muslim communities where anyone could develop a 'warped' interpretation of Islam, rendering all Muslims as potential terrorists in waiting. Secondly, that signs of radicalisation and extremism were racially coded; in other words, radicalisation was another word for Muslim difference construed as threatening, excessive or pathological. Thirdly, the thing being threatened through radicalisation was an unspoken white British nation, which served as a reference point for what was considered to be a 'normal', non-radical and non-extremist identity.

Characterisations of Muslim difference through Prevent should be understood not solely as religious but also as rooted in a concurrent British history of racialisation and colonialism. Muslims are raced through a mixture of strategies that draw on ideas about religious, cultural and biological differences which converge to produce an idea of what Salman Sayyid calls 'Muslimness'.[64] This understanding of Muslim difference is supplemented by a strong imaginary about the radical otherness of so-called 'Muslim' practices. From this perspective, Prevent is fundamentally concerned with the government of Black and brown bodies which exhibit signs of Muslimness.[65] In this setting, community cohesion or how to make Muslims more like 'us' was considered a form of counter-radicalisation, sitting alongside more coercive counter-terrorism measures. Prevent would not only entail referring people to de-radicalisation panels but an array of practices (explored in Chapter 2) aimed at teaching, regulating and disciplining Muslim populations into being 'good' British citizens. It is through the designation of collective responsibility that a racially marked Muslim community became seen as threatening to Britain, which itself is implicitly constructed as a white nation.

## Racial conceits

Trevor Phillips' view that all Muslims should be judged collectively as adherents of Islam reveals that attempts to separate critiques of Islam from critiques of Muslims are a political and rhetorical conceit. Free speech defences of Islamophobia usually rest on a neat division between critiques of Islam as a set of beliefs (acceptable) and criticisms of Muslims as a diverse group of people (less acceptable). However, this division is less sustainable when we consider how, in Britain, Islam was and remains read through the racial lens of colonialism as a despotic, intolerant and 'wild' faith. Such colonial racial tropes have gained new purchase through the global War on Terror which has been awash with orientalist ideas about Islam as a 'backwards' religion.

The racialisation of Islam has necessarily meant the corresponding racialisation of the 'Muslim'. The process of racialisation, the means through which something or someone is made a vessel for racialised characteristics, is not a reflection of the faith or its practitioners. Racism tells us about the anxieties, aspirations and intent of the racist and not about the 'race' with whom society might be preoccupied in that moment. Farid Hafez has argued that the prevalence of Islamophobia in Eastern European states where Muslim populations are vanishingly small, speaks largely to the powerful imaginary nature of racisms. Muslims do not even have to be *present* in Poland or Hungary in order to be framed as a problem of integration or security seeking to subvert Europe from within.[66]

When Phillips speaks about 'Islam' he is speaking about an idea of Islam as a monolithic entity, rather than a complex theological tradition with distinctive schools of thought, traversed by common and sometimes competing histories. This is what the anthropologist Talal Asad means when he describes Islam as 'discursive tradition'.[67] When Phillips speaks about Muslims he is not really speaking about a diverse group of people or their varied lived experience. He is speaking about an idea of Muslims. This is the racial conceit upon which Prevent is also built.

# 2

# *Domesticating Muslims*

In 2014, the Education Secretary Michael Gove ordered two parallel inquiries into a group of schools in Birmingham following the circulation of an anonymous letter alleging an 'Islamist takeover'. Later dubbed the Trojan Horse affair, the letter outlined that some 25 schools were being targeted by local extremists in a systematic attempt to 'Islamise' schools. The national press led with frenzied headlines regarding secret jihadist plots and Islamist takeovers, adding further fuel to the fire.[1] Despite the fact the letter was widely viewed as a hoax and had been dismissed by Birmingham City Council, its ramifications remained devastating. Park View School, Nansen Primary and Golden Hillock secondary run by Park View Educational Trust (PVET) were all put into special measures despite two of them having previously been rated as 'outstanding' by Ofsted. Muslim school teachers were fired from their jobs and the predominantly Muslim children attending these schools continue to deal with the stigma generated by lurid press reporting and multiple state interventions.[2]

The Trojan Horse affair is yet another example of how colonial ideas about a Muslim conspiracy were invoked and adapted for the context of postcolonial Britain. In fact, in his book *Celsius 7/7* Gove had articulated views about an Islamic takeover years earlier, in a chapter ironically entitled 'Trojan Horse' echoing Cold War fears of Trotskyist entryism into the British state apparatus.[3] The idea of a Muslim conspiracy enabled a set of political interventions that we can now make sense of through the idea of 'domestication'. Neither of the two inquiries into these schools – one conducted by the schools regulator Ofsted[4] and the other by Peter Clarke, a former police officer who had led the Metropolitan Police's Counter Terrorism Command – found any evidence of either radicalisation or terrorism.[5] Rather, the attention of government, Ofsted and Peter Clarke came to rest on the idea of an exclusionary Muslim identity being promoted in the schools and a failure to prepare Muslim school children for life in diverse Britain.[6]

While the framework of surveillance and Prevent referrals for children as young as four dominate critical thinking about the impacts of counter-radicalisation, domestication broadens how we can think about the functions of security policy. Domestication strategies for bringing nature, animals and plant life under control and into the service of man have historically also extended to human life. Ghassan Hage invites us to reflect on the distinctly colonial logics of domestication which were closely connected to the making of nation states conceived of as domestic spaces.[7] Hage shows how the primary function of the new nation states was to produce feelings of belonging or 'homeliness' by arbitrating on who does and does not belong.[8] 'Race', gender, class, sexuality and disability all serve as crucial vectors through which ideas about belonging and exclusion are made.

Trojan Horse was read as a failure to domesticate Muslim populations into the white British nation. While there was no actual evidence of either radicalisation or terrorism, there was still considerable alarm about so-called 'Muslim' practices which threatened the homeliness of white Britain like a cuckoo in the nest. Birmingham City Council was singled out for not addressing concerns raised in the letter, which had initially been viewed as an attempt to cause community tension. In his investigation however, Clarke argued that it was irrelevant whether or not the letter was a hoax because despite containing 'factual inaccuracies' it also contained a 'truth' which should have been investigated.[9] Clarke notes that while there was no evidence of a systematic Islamist takeover, there should have been enough concern about the actions of Muslim governors, teachers and parents to warrant further exploration. Namely, these were related to accusations of gender segregation, the teaching of homophobic material, religious intolerance (i.e. 'banning' Christmas) and promoting an anti-Western ethos.

This chapter explores the ways in which Prevent has functioned to domesticate Britain's Muslim populations to white Britain. These practices of domestication can be divided into three distinct but interrelated categories: the pedagogical, the regulatory and the disciplinary. The pedagogical refers to how Prevent has been in the business of teaching Muslims how to interpret and practice their faith in a way that does not conflict with being a good British citizen. Pedagogy has been at the heart of Prevent's work from the production of citizenship material for Muslim children to its culmination in the instruction of British values. The discussion then moves on to the regulatory aspects of Prevent, or the ways in which the management of Muslim populations has occurred through institutional and bureaucratic means. This section focuses on the transformations that have occurred within Britain's mosques and their co-option into the third sector as registered charities. Finally, the chapter concludes by exploring the disciplinary aspects of pre-emptive counter-terrorism exemplified in the Prevent Duty. The duty effectively introduces the everyday bordering of Muslim citizens across a range of state institutions by compelling workers in public sector institutions such as schools, colleges, and hospitals, to monitor and report individuals who may be 'vulnerable' to radicalisation.

## Teaching Muslims

The Trojan Horse scandal revealed racialised anxieties about how Muslim school children were being educated in ways deemed threatening to the borders of white Britain. But the emphasis on educating Muslims in how to correctly interpret and practice their faith was central to early Prevent work. If the measure of being radicalised was exhibiting a 'distorted and unrepresentative version of the Islamic faith' then early Prevent work placed a premium on promoting an acceptable version of Islam. The lion's share of early Prevent funding went to activities categorised as 'debate, discussion, forum' and 'general education'.[10] There were a broad range of pedagogical activities funded by Prevent, including study circles for Muslims to discuss all matters Islamic. For example, the Radical Middle Way road show that began touring after 7/7 was described as 'a series of talks aimed at steering Muslims away from extremism by clearing up misconceptions and misinterpretations of the Koran.'[11] Pedagogical initiatives were aimed at teaching Muslims to practice their faith in a way that was conducive to life in Britain and not threatening to it.

For Sergei Prozorov this is a form of liberal governance which relies on teaching citizens how to practise the freedom bestowed on them by the state in an appropriate manner.[12] British Muslims are being taught how to use the freedom they have been granted by virtue of their British citizenship in a way which doesn't violate or call into question the legitimacy of the state. Prevent-funded activities, from the establishment of theological study circles to the creation of youth forums for debates on being Muslim, can be understood through this prism of pedagogy. These activities, led predominantly by Muslim organisations and individuals, also reflect the idea of collective responsibility discussed in Chapter 1, once again placing the onus on British Muslims to take ownership of radicalisation and extremism.

### Citizenship education

While the teaching of British values has drawn considerable scholarly attention, the roots of this approach lie in the broader pedagogical initiatives ushered in through Prevent. The rationale for these efforts was to instruct Muslims as to how they could be good citizens. Early Prevent guidance argued that this could be achieved by the following:

> using opportunities in the school curriculum – and in colleges, universities and elsewhere – to convey a deeper understanding of faith, history and culture working particularly with the Muslim community to help strengthen religious understanding among young people and in particular support an understanding of citizenship in an Islamic context. This may include work in partnership with Islamic institutions such as mosque schools.[13]

Citizenship material for mosque schools emerged as a key focal point in Prevent delivery, with various state funded initiatives popping up. These included the Nasiha Project in Bradford, the Building Bridges initiative in Pendle, the Madrassah Citizenship Programme in Barnet and the more national in scope ICE Project.[14] The purpose of these projects was to 'provide young Muslims with a better understanding of how their faith is compatible with wider shared values and with living in Britain.'[15] Furthermore, the projects were described as 'community-led' and approved by 'local Islamic scholars' in an attempt to generate legitimacy among young Muslims.[16]

The wider context of citizenship education in the UK and its prominence under the New Labour government is also relevant. In 2002, following on from the Crick Report, citizenship education became part of the compulsory national curriculum. The introduction of citizenship education was a response to the crisis in the legitimacy of democratic institutions reflected in low voter turnout, social inequalities and political apathy.[17] Children between the ages of 11–16 would be taught about British parliamentary democracy, the rule of law, civic engagement and living in ethnically and religiously diverse societies. A key aspect of this work was the recognition that the UK is composed of a 'plurality of nations, cultures, ethnic identities and religions'.[18] Citizenship education would serve to create common ground in a Britain that was both a product of its colonial history and a member of the EU.

It is unsurprising that citizenship education was mobilised as part of counter-radicalisation work, because it was already a part of the political zeitgeist. Radicalisation and terrorism were read as part of the same milieu of social problems as social exclusion. However, they were considered to be more politically urgent due to the racial anxieties attached to them. At this time debates about British identity were becoming increasingly pivotal in political discourse in light of the riots in the north of England, 7/7 and panic around immigration. Policy makers began expressing increasing unease about what makes Britain 'British' and a view that 'society is coming unstuck at the edges and is increasingly lacking ties that bind all citizens together'.[19] While New Labour began its term in office with something of a commitment to multicultural politics this became increasingly ambivalent until it finally gave way to what Sivamohan Valluvan calls the 'clamour of nationalism'.[20]

The citizenship material which sought to instruct Muslim school children about how to be British emerged from a context of racial tensions and contestations around national identity. This was embodied in Gordon Brown's call to think about what constitutes British values and to cultivate pride in being British, which culminated in his later clarion call of 'British jobs for British workers'. By attempting to stress a more coherent national identity in response to the racial anxieties attached to radicalisation, citizenship education would serve to sharpen the boundaries between the 'inside' and 'outside' of Britain.[21] Citizenship education would teach Muslim children about how to be good *British* Muslims and set national limits on their identity as members of the global Ummah. It would do this by prescribing forms of appropriate political participation and ostensibly creating a sense of national belonging.

An example of this approach was the government funded ICE Project created by the anti-racist educationalist, Maurice Irfan Coles. The project produced 50 lessons on citizenship which were aimed at Muslim children between the ages of 9–14 being taught in mosque schools and in some primary and secondary schools. The lessons were designed through consultation with different Muslim scholars and organisations, cutting across different Islamic traditions and schools of thought. The lessons were 'validated by a wide range of Muslima ulama'[22] and trialled in London, Bradford, Kirklees, Leicester, Oldham, Rochdale and Bristol. The ICE Project is underwritten by the simple logic that being a 'good Muslim within the context of the United Kingdom means being a good and active citizen.'[23]

The pedagogical material teaches that there is no necessary conflict between Islam and British democracy and to equip students with the ability to 'counter extremist ideologies'.[24] The lessons are divided into four themes: democracy, justice, law and order; rights and responsibilities; identity and diversity; and the skills of citizenship.[25] The compatibility of Islam with British democracy and being a good citizen are established in three ways. The first is by clarifying who has the power to guide Muslims, thereby precluding radical and conservative Muslim voices who dissent from ideas of democracy, equality and active citizenship. The second is by re-interpreting Islamic theological traditions through liberal values such as tolerance, diversity and inquiry to guide 'correct' interpretations of Islam. Third, the lessons are concerned with territorialising the beliefs and practices of Muslims, to encourage concern for country, city, and community as opposed to the Ummah.[26]

The idea of citizenship is central to the inculcation of national values, and it is the space in which attempts are made to create common ground between differently positioned groups of people in Britain. The fact that the ICE Project was produced with Muslim children in mind chimes with Valluvan's contention that those citizens racialised as other in Western societies must learn how to be more civically minded. The reinterpretation of Islam through the ICE Project promotes a British Islam that excludes schools of thought deemed threatening to Britishness. Even though the lessons encourage Muslim children to enquire about their faith, the kinds of answers they can come up with are predetermined through citizenship education. This reinterpretation of Islam through liberal values also serves to reproduce some of the paradoxes of liberal politics. Muslims are tolerated and thus 'free' to practise their faith – but only in politically prescribed ways.

## British values

The end of New Labour's term in office was marked by the arrival of the Conservative-led coalition government in 2011, signalling a shift away from citizenship education and an increasing emphasis towards promoting British values. Education secretary Michael Gove exhibited a particular hostility towards citizenship education, whose place within the national curriculum was threatened by a review of topics considered to be 'pseudo subjects'.[27] Citizenship education survived the review but was reduced and modified in scope with a reduced emphasis on political literacy, negotiating multiple identities or civic engagement. Rather, citizenship lessons focused on financial responsibility, volunteering and knowledge about financial services and products.[28] This in part reflected the spirit of the Conservative Party manifesto, which advocated for austerity measures as a response to the effects of the Global Financial Crisis of 2008.

Political literacy, democratic participation and active citizens were not central to the political vision of the Education Secretary or his government. This might seem curious, given that the tensions which emerged from the Trojan Horse Affair were to do with the supposed 'failure' of schools to prepare Muslim children for life in a Britain characterised by its commitment to democratic values. Redoubling efforts around citizenship education designed to teach young people about the benefits of active citizenship, as well as reflecting on how to navigate various claims of identity, would seem a valuable tool in this work. However, the government instead chose to promote national values which were articulated in response to racial anxieties about Muslims. British values are less to do with the individual values themselves, which were already part of citizenship education, but about marking out the difference between 'Britains' and 'extremist Muslims'.

'Extremism' was defined by HM's Government as:

vocal or active opposition to fundamental British values, including democracy, the rule of law, individual liberty and mutual respect and tolerance of different faiths and beliefs. We also include in our definition of extremism calls for the death of members of our armed forces, whether in this country or overseas.[29]

'British values', meanwhile, were enshrined through counter-terrorism legislation and were aimed at securing a British national identity on the terrain of security policy. British values as outlined in the Counter-Terrorism and Security Act (2015) were defined as democracy; the rule of law; individual liberty; mutual respect for and tolerance of those with different faiths and beliefs, and for those without faith. While it's difficult to ascertain what is uniquely 'British' about these values, the trend of asserting national values and identity as a response to the threat of terrorism and radicalisation was also in evidence in states such as Sweden and France.

Following on from the Trojan Horse affair, British values became part of Ofsted inspection processes, with schools being judged on how effectively these values are being promoted. Robert Harris argues that the teaching of British values has in effect 'superseded' citizenship education in determining ideas of national identity and belonging.[30] While the ICE Project was an attempt to conjure up a 'good' British Muslim citizen, British values represents a move towards instructing all children about who belongs and who does not. These developments in education can be understood as a more explicit attempt to inculcate racialised national values. While citizenship material for Muslim children was troubling on its own terms, the promotion of British values marked a move away from working with Muslim partners towards a fully top-down approach to marking out national space.

Whereas citizenship education had stressed the idea of a Britain enmeshed in the world, connected to the EU and Commonwealth countries, British values promoted what Hugh Starkey calls a 'narrow nationalistic' idea of Britain.[31] Starkey goes on to argue that British values 'appears as a coercive attempt to require schools to privilege a predetermined national narrative over a perspective that includes the local and the global and allows space for discussing different experiences and traditions of the national narrative'.[32] The national narrative promoted through British values is one that is premised on imperial amnesia and white supremacy. Christine Winter and China Mills argue Britain's colonial history calls into question the idea that freedom, tolerance, rule or law and democracy were universal values from which all Britons benefited.[33] The British Empire was characterised by its unequal treatment of British colonial subjects based on racial differentiation.

This means historically British values were not universally applicable but were denied to colonised populations who were regarded as incapable or unworthy of governing themselves. Furthermore, colonial violence was advanced and legitimated through legal instruments such as the rule of law. Democratic rights including the ability to vote, the right to political association and the right to free speech were not extended to colonised populations and were actively repressed in the face of mounting anti-colonial movements.[34] Slavery, racism, and exploitation were all constitutive features of the British Empire which is not acknowledged in the story of Britain advanced through British values. To summarise, the idea that Britain is home to freedom, rule of law and tolerance rests on not only an incomplete reading of history but a reading of history which erases the realities of white supremacist colonial violence. British values serve to remake an idea of Britishness as whiteness by marking out which citizens belong, and which ones are suspect based on racial differentiation.

British values are racially coded because they have developed through particular concerns about the supposed threat posed by Muslim citizens. Consequently, British values uphold what Claire Crawford calls 'native (white British) cultural norms and mores only, as evidenced by David Cameron when he asserted that [Fundamental British Values] are as British as the Union Flag, as football, (and) as fish and chips'.[35] It is not so much an attachment to individual values for their own sake which is being encouraged – to be tolerant, to centre claims of freedom, to obey the law – but rather an unquestioning devotion to Britain itself as a white nation. This contradiction is easily observed in the case of white Britons who do not uphold individual British values but are not considered to have breached the borders of the nation. For example, when over half the Conservative Party voted against legalising gay marriage, a cornerstone of David Cameron's modernising agenda for the party, this was considered a personal embarrassment for the Prime Minister but not a cause for alarm around a lack of commitment to equality. Not long after that, the schools caught up in the Trojan Horse Affair were berated for promoting homophobia to their Muslim students.

### Regulating Muslims

While the pedagogical aspects of Prevent pertained to teaching Muslim children how to interpret and practice their faith, regulation is concerned with creating the right conditions in spaces where Muslims circulate. In the early 2000s, mosques in Britain occupied a particularly important role in discourses about radicalisation and terrorism. They came to be regarded as ungoverned spaces in which dangerous Muslim difference could flourish. This view was best exemplified by the controversies which engulfed Finsbury Park Mosque in the early days of the War on Terror. In 2003, the mosque was raided by 150 police officers in riot gear in relation to the so-called 'Wood Green ricin plot'. The plot was painted by politicians and the press as that of a transnational al-Qaeda cell based in London planning a large bio-chemical attack. But the trial of the five Algerian men at the centre of the 'plot' saw four acquittals for terrorism charges and the emergence of the fact police had not actually found any ricin during their raids.

Lawrence Archer and Fiona Bawdon describe the case as 'built on sand, based on a case riddled with misinformation' which was crucial in bolstering the US and UK case of the War on Terror.[36] Nevertheless, the consequences of this case and intelligence extracted from detainees in Guantanamo Bay detention centre through methods including torture had far reaching implications for other mosques. The WikiLeaks Guantanamo Files reinforced the idea that mosques in Britain were an important part of a global 'jihadist' network. US interrogators claimed that Finsbury Park Mosque in London has a history of serving as an attack planning and propaganda production base. US intelligence meanwhile considered the mosques a key recruitment facility for al-Qaeda associated movements, as well as a hub for raising funds and moving them around globally.[37] Regent's Park Mosque, East London Mosque and Finsbury Park Mosque all feature in the Guantanamo Files, depicted as part of a transnational jihadi web.

At this time, the figure of Abu Hamza al-Masri came to serve as a lightning rod for conversations about the relationship between mosques, radicalisation and terrorism. Al-Masri stood accused of radicalising young people through his sermons and of being engaged in an effort to 'takeover' Finsbury Park Mosque. He was eventually prosecuted for soliciting murder and was subsequently extradited to the US. The controversies surrounding Finsbury Park underlined to the New Labour government that mosques were largely outside the formal structures of state governance. Historically, mosques in Britain were run by and for Muslim communities and established along varying ethnic, national and theological lines and traditions.[38]

Initially the New Labour government attempted to introduce legislation expanding its policing powers over mosques, but this attempt was thwarted. Instead the focus was placed on bringing mosques into state regulation. This would be accomplished by the establishment of the national Mosque and Imams National Advisory Board (MINAB), designed to improve governing standards in mosques. Part of MINAB's work was to encourage mosques to register as charities, bringing them into the oversight of the Charity Commission (CC). While the idea for an independent governing body for mosques emerged from Muslim civil society itself, its co-option into counter-radicalisation efforts is undeniable. MINAB was funded through Prevent and facilitated by the Department for Communities and Local Government (DCLG), working alongside four Muslim organisations: the Muslim Council of Britain, British Muslim Forum, Muslim Association of Britain and the al-Khoei Foundation. The work of MINAB and the CC went hand in hand and helps explain how the work of Prevent was extended through charitable status.

## MINAB

MINAB was established as a charitable organisation in 2007 to oversee the reform of mosques and Islamic centres under the umbrella of 'counter-radicalisation' and to provide guidance and oversight to this process. The guiding principles of MINAB stressed its composition as an 'independent' and 'non-sectarian' body which represents 'the diversity of Islam'.[39] MINAB's strategy was two-fold: promoting good corporate governance in mosques and turning mosques into community hubs. Key to this was the training and accreditation of imams. These reforms were intended to enable mosques to function as more than places of worship but also as locations that could in turn regulate Muslim citizens.

### Promoting good corporate governance

Strengthening standards of government with a focus on good corporate governance became a core part of mosque reform. Good corporate governance emerged from major corporate scandals in the 1980s involving companies such as Coloroll, Polly Peck International (PPI) and the Bank of Credit and Commerce International (BCCI). The collapse of these companies, which involved vast hidden debts, theft and other financial crimes led to a rethinking of the way businesses were governed. A series of investigations led by the UK government culminated in the establishment of a Code for Good Corporate Governance for businesses (UKCGC) and these standards eventually made their way into the governance of the public and charity sector. Good corporate governance was about creating the right regulatory conditions, such as financial transparency, in which companies and organisations could grow while also being held accountable.

The movement of good governance practices from the private sector to the public and charity sectors saw the instantiation of a business model way of working, as reflected in the codes of conduct which regulate central government departments.[40] This idea of an optimum level of regulation also informed the CC's counter-radicalisation strategy and its oversight of financial transparency in particular. The concern regarding mosques and terrorism financing has seen the CC investigating numerous Muslim charities since 2008.[41] As an intermediary between the state and historically autonomous mosques, MINAB led the drive to encourage mosques to register as charities, co-opting them into state regulatory structures. MINAB's role was also to bring about regulatory changes through which mosques would develop accountable and strong leadership to prevent financial abuse.

The crisis in Finsbury Park Mosque generated political anxiety surrounding the robustness of internal leadership structures, which MINAB's good corporate governance sought to address. MINAB encouraged its members to democratically elect its mosque committee in order to provide legitimate leadership. Organisations such as Urban Nexus, Faith Associates and Oak Community Development developed training events to assist mosques in the work of leadership training. For instance, the Beacon Mosque Programme designed by Urban Nexus was designed to deliver mosques with 'infrastructure, governance and confidence through providing training to key individuals in management committees'.[42] The programme focused on creating leadership for Muslims, which encompassed an examination of leadership traits, behaviours, and styles to initiate a 'journey of life-long learning and reflection' among participants.[43]

Oak Community Development and Faith Associates also produced a 'Management Guide for Mosques & Islamic Centres' to help reju-venate leadership in mosques.[44] It offers a step-by-step guide on how a mosque committee can be elected and the kinds of characteristics Muslims should look for in their trustees, including piety, trustwor-thiness, commitment, knowledge and skills. These training materials – aimed at achieving the kind of regulatory changes envisaged by the CC – were however, only one aspect of mosque reform. At a more fun-damental level mosques were also regarded as a space through which Muslim citizens at large could be governed.

### Mosques as inclusive community hubs and imam training

MINAB was premised on the idea that 'there is huge potential for mosques as agents for the community and social development. The role of community leadership from the imams to the mosque officials in motivating, educating, guiding and involving (the) Muslim com-munities cannot be overestimated'.[45] From this perspective, mosques were conceived as community hubs, which would guide the conduct of Muslim worshipers. MINAB stressed the idea that mosques had a duty to instil a sense of civic responsibility among the faithful, emphasising the obligations of Muslim worshippers to wider society. Civic respon-sibility was seen as a way of fostering community cohesion among Muslims and non-Muslims and creating resistance against the lures of radicalisation.

The idea of civic responsibility was communicated and legitimated through the Islamic concept of *Khidmah* meaning 'service to humanity': 'The Qur'an and other Islamic sacred texts call upon Muslims to be active citizens involved in the affairs of their fellow citizens and in con-tributing to wider society'.[46] As with the citizenship education material designed for Muslim children, reinterpreting Qur'anic and other scholarly sources through liberal political concepts was a marked feature of early Prevent, seeking to domesticate Muslim populations to the white British home. While MINAB's drive to make mosques more inclusive for young people and women may have been long overdue, these reforms were undeniably located in concerns about radicalisation and the desire to regulate Muslim conduct.

The strength of connection between mosques and young people came under considerable scrutiny after 7/7. Young people were seen as more at risk of accepting radical iterations of Islam because they were being failed by community elders who were unable to understand and respond to their concerns. Moreover, as Naaz Rashid has shown, early Prevent cast Muslim women as 'peacemakers' who were not at risk of radicalisation.[47] Provisions for female worshippers in UK mosques was patchy and the absence of women was seen as a pre-condition of radicalisation. In making mosques more responsive to the needs of young people and women, it was hoped that the reach of mosque leaderships within Muslim communities would also expand to young people at risk of radicalisation and the Muslim woman who could help 'save' them.[48]

Central to the regulation of Muslim conduct was the figure of the appropriately trained and accredited imam who could guide their flock according to the mores of civic responsibility. While racist and ableist depictions of al-Masri came to dominate the popular imagination about imams 'gone wrong', the idea of the 'good' imam was taking shape in the parallel world of counter-radicalisation. However, notions of the role and significance of the imam were significantly shaped by the figure of the Christian priest around whom a congregation is amassed and awaiting instruction. Martin van Bruinessen and Stefano Allievi contend that the 'importance of imams has been exaggerated' to the extent they are expected to be leaders or spokespeople.[49] Being an imam was often a voluntary part-time position, as well as being one poorly paid and lacking in social esteem.

Sophie Gilliat-Ray, Mansur Ali and Stephen Pattinson argue that 'there is no tradition of institutionalised chaplaincy in Islam, there is implicit theology that supports and encourages what might be called "pastoral care".'[50] Imams have historically performed roles in rites of passage such as births, marriages and deaths rather than playing the role of the shepherd guiding a flock, which is so central to Christian traditions. Finally, the issue of English language skills was also flagged as a potential barrier in the instruction of Britain's Muslims. However, the prominence of imams in public life had been increasing prior to 7/7. This was partly because of changes within the delivery of public sector services which emphasises diversity and inclusion as well as the confidence of Muslim communities themselves in demanding provisions.[51]

MINAB's attempts to introduce regulation for imam training and accreditation reflects the idea of what Jonathan Birt calls 'good' and 'bad' imams. Birt writes,

> The good imam is now to embody civic virtues, interfaith tolerance, professional managerial and pastoral skills, possibly become involved in intercity regeneration, work as an agent of national integration (most importantly on behalf of his unruly flock), and wage a jihad against extremism. By contrast, the bad imam has become the agent of divisive cultural and religious alterity to be deterred by multiplying bureaucratic hurdles, defamed, deported or imprisoned.[52]

The purpose of regulation can be understood through the twin ideas of professionalising and territorialising the imam. Professionalising imams has involved providing them with English language support, sending them on training courses and up-skilling throughout their careers, thereby making them fit for their pastoral roles. Territorialising imams – or making them more relevant to a British context – was motivated by the idea of imams as lacking adequate knowledge of Britain and being unable to guide their younger constituents. The provision of English language training and formalised training was in part, at least, a way to domesticate imams to the British context.

## Disciplining Muslims

While ideas about pedagogy and regulation dominated early Prevent, there is a marked shift to a more starkly disciplinary approach from 2011 onwards. The Conservative-led coalition moved away from working alongside co-opted Muslim partners in the instruction and regulation of Muslim populations and towards a blunter version of domestication. The shift can be explained by the Conservative Party's critique of early Prevent as wasteful of public money in an election fought on the terrain of fiscal responsibility following the Global Financial Crisis (GFC). While it was a myth that public overspending was the cause of the GFC, this claim allowed the Conservatives to enact policies of austerity that could also be seen in relation to counter-terrorism. More importantly, there was also an emergent view that Prevent funding was finding its way to 'extremist organisations'.[53] But, by the new government's own admission there was 'no evidence to indicate widespread, systematic or deliberate funding of extremist groups'.[54] This detail did not dampen conspiratorial ideas of Muslim 'entryism' into state institutions propagated by Michael Gove and Policy Exchange, an influential right-wing think tank he helped to co-found.[55]

Gove's subsequent clarion call to 'drain the swamp' of Islamist extremism was heeded with alacrity by the new Prime Minister David Cameron. In 2011, Cameron's speech at the Munich Security Conference advocated for a muscular liberal approach to counter-radicalisation.[56] According to Cameron, terrorism was not a symptom of legitimate political grievances, social exclusion, or poverty. Rather, terrorism was the product of cultural separatism allowed to flourish in a setting where state multiculturalism has weakened a strong collective British identity. The promotion and policing of a coherent national identity articulated around liberal values branded as uniquely 'British', including free speech, democracy, rule of law and equality was the new antidote to terrorism.

A muscular liberal approach meant that the practices of working with co-opted formerly 'extremist' Muslim partners or funding Muslim community-based initiatives characteristic of early Prevent fell out of favour. Instead, Prevent would be put to the service of propagating a white national identity through British Values and proactively policing their transgression. These changes were embodied in the Counter-Terrorism and Security Act in 2015 which brought about the Prevent Duty (PD). The PD places a statutory obligation on the part of specific institutions to prevent individuals from being radicalised and on schools to teach British values. The discussion earlier in this chapter on citizenship education showed that British values are racially marked by their opposition to 'Muslim' values of the kind admonished by Cameron.

At a moment when resistance to Prevent was growing, the PD offered an opportunity for rebranding in which policymakers and practitioners could argue that all forms of extremism would be targeted. Furthermore, by implementing the PD as a form of safeguarding for those vulnerable to radicalisation, the explicit attention to Muslims and Islam that characterised early Prevent was being hidden away. However, training frontline workers such as teachers and doctors to decide who is an extremist threat based on 'gut instincts' relies on tacit racist assumptions about the Muslim threat to white Britain. The final part of the chapter explores the erasure by the backdoor of the racial violence central to Prevent which belongs to a much older colonial tradition of racism in Britain. The chapter concludes by setting out how the PD is an intensification of legally formalised racial bordering experienced by Muslims who have to prove their Britishness in order to show they are not extremist.

### The Prevent Duty

By the time the Conservative-led coalition came to power in 2011, there was a growing critique of Prevent as a policy which targets and stigmatises Muslim communities, with calls for an independent review. Early Prevent explicitly focused on Muslim populations but after 2011, the guidance emphasised attention to all forms of extremism. Coupled with the fact that the Home Office has never collected faith and ethnicity data for Prevent referrals beyond the ideological orientation of subjects such as 'Islamist' or 'right wing' – some may interpret the policy as neutral and to be applied when needed. The PD offered another way to neutralise criticisms by presenting counter-radicalisation as safeguarding, which is designed to protect the health, wellbeing and rights of vulnerable adults and children.

Attempts to erase the racial provenance of Prevent that are meant to counter accusations of Islamophobia fit with an older British colonial tradition of racial differentiation by the back door. Historically, the British Empire was able to postulate values of 'liberalism' and 'moderation' while also concealing the depth of racial violence lurking under the surface and often above it. The racism of the Belgian or German Empires is less contestable, because their open embrace of scientific racism meant the occupation of Congo or Tanzania was justified in terms of racial superiority. Scientific racism was the well from which their practices of colonial rule were rationalised and implemented. By contrast, the British Empire was understood by those governing it as a project of 'freedom, civilisation and liberalism' which was judged 'comparatively benign' alongside Belgian or German equivalents.[57]

Like all European empires, racism was at the heart of British colonialism, sitting alongside ideas of freedom and individual rights which were not extended to colonised people of colour. But practices of racial differentiation which marked colonial rule were generally not couched in terms of racial superiority. British colonial rule was administered through ideas of who had the capacity to bear rights and exercise their freedom in a civilised way. The attribution of 'individual characteristics' to differently racialised colonised populations was central in marking out who could be a bearer of rights and who could not.[58] Therefore, policies aimed at making racial differentiation were not necessarily rationalised in terms of scientific racism but in terms of the character of colonised populations. The PD bears the hallmarks of stealth racial differentiation by attributing characteristics to Muslim populations which mark them out as always potentially extremist by virtue of their faith and at risk of losing their rights.

The Workshop to Raise Awareness of Prevent (WRAP) training which is supposed to equip (among others) healthcare workers and educators with the capacity to identify those who are vulnerable to radicalisation bears the hallmarks of this approach. WRAP trainers emphasise the fact anyone can become a terrorist and the training material includes case studies of Muslim and far-right subjects. However, when the public health charity Medact interviewed NHS staff who received WRAP training some respondents argued the training was 'overly focused on Islam' with fleeting attention to the far-right and 'pandering to stereotypes' of Muslims.[59] Furthermore, the signs of radicalisation flagged in the training are only comprehensible in the context of narratives in early Prevent about the Muslim threat. For example, the idea that Muslims hold grievances about British foreign policy, are impacted by international conflicts and carry dangerous cultural and religious baggage.[60]

The framework of safeguarding also enables and conceals the racially discriminatory nature of the PD. In the absence of a clear criteria of who is at risk of radicalisation, frontline workers are actively empowered to make decisions about potential extremists based on gut instinct. As Shereen Fernandez, Rob Faure Walker and Tarek Younis have shown, gut instincts rely on 'racialised knowledge about risk and vulnerability'.[61] In other words, notions of who is radical or extreme are already embedded in wider British society through policies like Prevent, which teach people how Muslims are threatening to Britain. It is this racial knowledge which is activated when frontline workers are implored to 'trust your instincts'. The impact of the PD in healthcare shows the effects of decision-making which rests on racialised gut instincts. For example, Muslims were 8 times more likely to be referred to Prevent than non-Muslims.[62] The Medact report argued that this 'disproportionality is, at least in part a result of racial and religious discrimination'.[63]

Finally, the experience of healthcare workers doing the training is itself deeply instructive. In their interviews with NHS workers, Tarek Younis and Shushrat Jadhav found that those who had doubts about Prevent training feared expressing them in case they came to be viewed as 'terrorist sympathisers' with potential repercussions from higher powers.[64] Muslim healthcare workers in particular expressed both a fear of speaking out but also a sense they could be 'at the receiving end' of the training that was being given.[65] These workers understood they were the objects of racially marked suspicion even if they were afraid of vocalising such a view. In different ways, all the Muslim respondents in this study conveyed a sense of being marked out as the problem conveyed through WRAP training. Younis and Jadhav argue that such fear and self-censorship accompany the implementation of the PD in the NHS and as such, we cannot understand its impact without this wider knowledge.

## Prevent as racial bordering

From its inception, Prevent has been concerned with Muslim populations and the dangers they pose to white Britain. The domestication of Muslims rests on the teaching, regulation and enforcement of an acceptable and contained British Muslim identity. From this perspective we can think of Prevent as a set of practices which make borders of different kinds. This means that even though Muslims in Britain are citizens with the same notional rights and entitlements as other citizens, they are also subject to additional borders which call into question their belonging on a daily basis. Muslims are assumed to be not British enough, in need of instruction about how to be British and are all the while regarded as potential extremists ready to tip into violence directed against Britain.

While pedagogical and regulatory practices brought about new constraints in terms of how Muslim citizens should interpret and practise their faith and run their institutions, the PD has also imposed a more formalised border. By extending radicalisation prevention into spaces where public goods like healthcare and education are accessed, the state has introduced the border into classrooms, lecture theatres, GP's surgeries and hospitals. Doctors and nurses, teachers and lecturers are being mobilised as agents of the border, trained to detect extremists in the midst of students and patients they see every day. Those suspected of exhibiting signs of radicalisation are referred to Prevent, setting in motion a chain reaction of state intervention. Frontline workers are being trained to 'trust their gut instinct' in a context that is drenched with Islamophobic discourses about Muslim others. The next chapter looks at how the everyday racial bordering of Muslims brought about through Prevent renders their citizenship conditional.

# 3

# Conditional Citizenship

The growing importance attached to loyalty within core values (such as 'Britishness') as the citizen's reciprocal duty towards the state which grants the prize of citizenship.

Clive Walker QC[1]

Debates about counter-terrorism and citizenship have tended to focus on the inhumane practice of citizenship deprivation which has been normalised through the War on Terror.[2] The Borders and Nationality Act allows the state to remove the citizenship of naturalised British citizens even if it carries the prospect of statelessness and without having to notify the person in question. Critics argue that this legislation has the potential to impact six million Britons who have dual nationality or the (questionable) ability to become a citizen of another country.[3] The question of who is impacted by rules like this is hard to establish given how citizenship deprivation is a practice that unfolds behind closed doors and includes the state's use of secret courts and secret evidence. Nonetheless, according to the organisation Free Movement which provides legal advice to those impacted by immigration controls, 464 people have been deprived of their citizenship in the last 15 years, 175 of whom have been on the grounds of national security.[4]

In reality, the power of the state to enact citizenship deprivation on the grounds that it is 'conducive to public good' has been honed over a longer period of time and through successive pieces of immigration and nationality legislation. While this practice has been seen as one that primarily targets Muslim citizens charged with terrorism offences, the use of citizenship deprivation by the Home Secretary has expanded in the last 15 years. It is a particularly devastating example of a bordering practice because it entails making someone stateless, which leaves them outside of the legal boundaries of organised political, social and economic life. The gravity of this move, and the reason it attracts so much critical attention, reflects the fact that making someone stateless is illegal under international law. However, citizenship deprivation sits on a spectrum of bordering practices and is made possible by calling into question the belonging of Muslim citizens in everyday life.

This chapter looks at the mundane aspects of everyday racial bordering which foreground the possibility of deprivation by making the citizenship of Muslims conditional on upholding Britishness. This conditionality is reflected in how practices and attributes ascribed to Muslims – expressions of Muslimness – are mobilised to contest the rights and freedoms of Muslim citizens.[5] For example, the Conservative MP Nusrat Ghani argued that when she was sacked as a minister in 2020, a government whip told her that 'her Muslimness was raised as an issue' and that the fact she was 'a Muslim woman . . . was making colleagues uncomfortable'.[6]

This chapter begins by setting out the idea that while Muslims are citizens with the same formal rights as other Britons, their ability to 'act politically' is curtailed. This idea is explored further by looking at the gendered impacts of conditional citizenship on Muslim women and their ability to participate in public life. The chapter concludes by exploring how Muslim students in schools and universities engage in practices of self-censorship to pre-empt accusations of extremism that may lead to a Prevent referral. For Muslim populations, retaining British citizenship is increasingly premised on discarding any views and practices which might call into question their 'Britishness'.

*Citizenship and 'acting politically'*

In May 2016, the London Mayoral election reached its climax with the victory of the lawyer and Muslim MP, Sadiq Khan. The spectacle of the election campaign unfolded in the context of intensifying narratives describing Khan as 'radical' and 'extremist'.[7] His political views, the people he had defended in his professional life, and those he had associated with were all subject to headlines decrying his suitability to run the capital. His opponent, the Conservative MP Zac Goldsmith, expressed concerns that a Muslim would be responsible for overseeing the city's counter-terrorism strategy.[8] Khan was also accused of sharing platforms with 'extremists' who supported the Islamic State notably the imam Sulaiman Gani. David Cameron excoriated Gani in the House of Commons, claiming, 'He described women as subservient to men. He said that homosexuality was an unnatural act.'[9] It later transpired that Gani was an anti-Islamic State campaigner. Cameron issued an apology for the 'misunderstanding' regarding his potentially libellous descriptions of Gani as an IS supporter while being protected by parliamentary privilege.[10]

Khan won the election, however the hashtag #LondonHasFallen trended on Twitter that day.[11] In spite of his victory the election revealed the distinct challenges facing Muslims in Britain and their ability to exercise their citizenship in three important ways. Firstly, this case highlights how the supposed threats represented by Muslim citizens are not restricted to security concerns; neither Khan nor Gani were suspected of being involved in criminal or terrorist activity. Secondly, the statements made about both figures are revealing of how Muslim difference is understood in British political discourse. Gani was not only castigated for his alleged support for IS but also because of views ascribed to him on women and homosexuality. Such views are considered as evidence of the incompatibility of British values and Islam, and as a precursor to radicalisation and terrorism. Thirdly, participating in public and political life is increasingly conditional on passing tests of national loyalty whereby Muslims are compelled to demonstrate they are capable of upholding Britishness.

Debates in Britain have tended to focus on changes in legislation and how these have impacted the legal status of Muslim citizens. Citizenship deprivation is a good example of this. However, the informal impact of everyday racial borders embodied in Prevent and its connections with citizenship are less well understood. As Lee Jarvis and Michael Lister argue, 'anti-terrorism powers have impacted upon aspects of citizenship such as participation in public life far more dramatically than they have affected the status of formal rights.'[12] This chapter shows that Muslim populations are being made into conditional citizens prior to the enactment of formal citizenship deprivation. Engin Isin has argued that the ability to participate in public life should be understood as 'a right to being political'.[13] It is not simply enough to have citizenship when being able to exercise the rights of citizenship rests on being recognised as a full member of a political community. Simply put, even where Muslims have formal citizenship in Britain, their belonging to the nation is still regularly called into question, which prevents them from exercising their rights in the way white Britons do.

We know that through the Prevent strategy collective responsibility was conferred on Muslim communities for terrorist violence. From this perspective, the 2016 London mayoral election was an example of Sadiq Khan exercising his rights of citizenship by standing for election but having this right contested by opponents based on the Islamophobic idea that he was a traitor to the nation and terrorist sympathiser. Therefore, the idea of acting politically moves us away from the narrow view of citizenship as the legal category that determines full belonging to a state but that citizens have also to be accepted as belonging. The reasons why legal citizenship is not adequate for securing the belonging of all citizens can be seen in the history of citizenship. While the concept of citizenship has often been feted as a progressive one in European political history, it ultimately operates through the exclusion of those who are designated as not belonging to the nation.

Modern citizenship took shape through French revolutionary politics and the violent and protracted shift from divinely governed feudal orders to modern nation states. The idea of citizenship was crystallised in the *Declaration of the Rights of Man and of the Citizen* (1789), passed by the National Constituent Assembly in revolutionary France. This document outlined a radical new relationship between the rulers and the ruled. Immanuel Wallerstein has argued that after this French elites could no longer justify their positions through divine right but had to take recourse instead to 'the people' inhabiting discrete national spaces bound together in relations of political equality.[14] The boundaries of the nation state were therefore coterminous with 'the people'.[15] This is the founding myth of European nation states: France for the French, Germany for the Germans, Italy for the Italians and so on. For Roger Brubaker, citizenship is a political project with limited emancipatory potential precisely because it was based on this nationalist exclusion.[16] The ability to decide what makes a citizen was an exercise in power which operated along racial, gendered and class lines wherein property ownership was central.

Furthermore, for European powers who were also colonial powers, it was their colonised subjects who were important in defining the citizen at 'home'. Jack Harrington notes that the very idea of 'Europeans' was 'developed in the context of imperial citizenship'.[17] Isin provincializes citizenship as a product of 'European values' which existed in relation to colonial contexts that were deemed not to exemplify these traits.[18] The colonial experiences of European states varied substantially, as did their individual negotiations of citizenship. Nonetheless, the idea of a shared European identity is discernible and useful in thinking through the citizen/non-citizen dichotomy. Being European signified a racial, religious, cultural and economic superiority that was bound up in ideas of who could and could not be a citizen. For Barry Hindess, 'the imperialism of Western states and the development of citizenship within them had the effect of dividing the world into distinct kinds of populations: the citizen populations of Western states; non-citizen populations governed by these states'.[19]

These dividing effects of citizenship institutionalised ideas of racial, religious and national superiority as a part of European national identities. Those deemed non-citizens and non-European – usually racialised others seen as marginal or deviant – were populations who did not fit into the nation but whose exclusion allowed ideas of the nation to take shape. Similarly, Prevent has marked out Muslim populations as always potentially suspect, thereby allowing an idea of British values to emerge which sets out what a 'good' citizen looks like. This is a racialised process through which the otherness of Muslims is located in their religious beliefs and the fact that the majority of Muslims in Britain come from formerly colonised parts of the world. Therefore, the ability to act politically – to be seen as belonging to the nation and able to exercise the full rights of citizenship – requires doing so without having your capacity to do so called into question. Prevent inhibits the ability of Muslim citizens to act politically through the invitation to uphold British values – to be 'properly' British – or risk being labelled as radical or religious extremist. From here the chapter moves on to explore how the ability of Muslim women and children to act politically has been circumscribed through Prevent and its articulation of what it means to be British.

## Muslim women

When David Cameron gave his Munich Security speech in 2011, his test to 'properly judge' whether Muslim organisations should receive public funding was 'do they believe in universal human rights – including for women and people of other faiths?'[20] He describes how the failure to 'confront the horrors of forced marriage' was an example of a policy of state multiculturalism in which the tolerance for practices which 'run completely counter to our values' was evident.[21] Through Prevent, Muslim women were cast as victims of male Muslim violence in the same way as wider British society but also as potential allies in the War on Terror. Naaz Rashid has shown that Muslim women were understood as victims in need of saving but also mobilised as peaceful agents of change, who only needed to be empowered to challenge terrorism and radicalisation.[22] If we think of Islamophobia as a form of anti-Muslim racism which casts Muslims as adherents of a backwards faith, then gendered Islamophobia is how this racial violence is mediated through gender politics.[23]

Lila Abu Lughod has argued that saving Muslim women from barbaric Muslim men was a key idea which helped to justify the wider global War on Terror.[24] Islam came to be invoked as a backwards religion which treated women as objects of control and the rights of women with contempt. For instance, the invasion of Afghanistan was not simply to remove the Taliban, but also to free Muslim women. Gargi Bhattacharyya explains that the use of 'feminist rhetoric' came to serve as a 'symbolic marker in the struggle between "us" and "them" . . . and on the depiction of Western culture as being typified by multicultural tolerance'.[25] In claiming gender equality as a marker of Western civilisation and the War on Terror as an exercise in tremendous military power, asymmetrical violence and death was branded as being in the service of female emancipation. It is precisely this gender emancipatory promise which also runs through Prevent and its co-option of gender equality as a marker of Britishness.

Gender equality is a characteristic of the 'good' British citizen and gender inequality is a marker of those who fall outside of Britishness. Cameron's reference to forced marriage and the later emphasis on Female Genital Mutilation (FGM) came to be seen as signs of Muslimness and markers of being unBritish. Captured under the umbrella of Honour Based Abuse (HBA), such activities are described as a 'collection of practices, which are used to control behaviour within families or other social groups to protect perceived cultural and religious beliefs and/or honour'.[26] Patriarchal violence and misogyny were located outside the British body politic and cast as attributes of Muslim men. Any barriers that Muslim women might encounter within Britain in getting work, education or entering into political participation were seen as emerging from within their communities. The next section looks at how the co-option of gender equality into Prevent and positioning of Muslim women as either victims of Muslim men, or as allies who uphold British values, limits their ability to act politically.

The idea of empowering Muslim women, what Rashid calls the 'Empowering Muslim Women discourse' (EMW), has always been an important aspect of Prevent, with funding going to initiatives that promoted this goal.[27] In addition to using Prevent funding for local initiatives, the National Muslim Women's Advisory Group (NMWAG) was also established to guide the efforts of central government.[28] The logic of EMW was that by 'fixing' gender relations within Muslim communities, Muslim women could be mobilised as agents of Prevent and in the process be saved from the common scourge of the Muslim man. These ideas were made explicit in relation to Prevent by government minister Hazel Blears:

There are at least 800,000 Muslim women living in Britain today. They have a unique viewpoint on the challenges faced by the communities they live in – whether that is the threat of violent extremism, anti-social behaviour, or young people feeling isolated and disengaged. They are also uniquely placed to solve these problems, challenging unacceptable behaviour and supporting those in need. Unfortunately, all too often their voice goes unheard. Some don't have the confidence or skills to speak up in forums dominated by men.[29]

Rashid notes that critiques of unelected and male dominated organisations which claimed to 'represent' Muslim communities could also be levelled at the NMWAG. While there could be no doubt about the experience or skills many Muslim women brought to the role, the part they were asked to play was in delivering pre-determined and under resourced projects. Furthermore, Whitehall itself was felt by members of the NMWAG to be a marginalising work context, where the empowerment of Muslim women was aligned to aims of counter-terrorism policy. This constricted Muslim women from speaking on a full range of issues which impacted on their communities, but which fell outside of the Prevent agenda. While the subject of FGM, honour-based violence and empowerment were 'in', pervasive conditions of economic inequality facing Muslims were not.

Rashid notes 'Muslim women were only intelligible in the political arena if they fit certain norms'.[30] As one participant in the programme said, 'you can talk about the veil, . . . [but] if you want to discuss any other issues, you know I mean the credit crunch, anything, then you're not allowed a voice because what could you possibly know'.[31] Simply put, the Muslim women working in this area had their ability to act politically – or to speak to issues outside of the ones which had been ascribed to them as victims or agents of change – severely constrained. They were to serve as 'gatekeepers, as mothers, as sisters' rather than 'active economic participants and citizens'.[32] The starkness of this constraint to act politically was best embodied by the fact the groups and individuals critical of Prevent were not seen as the 'right' kind of voice or 'representative' of the Muslim community. Rashid concludes that, 'within the category of 'Muslim women' certain voices were also louder (or more often heard) than others; this was often connected to their particular areas of expertise or that they were uncritical more broadly of the Prevent agenda'.[33]

While Prevent ostensibly sought to 'empower' and 'free' Muslim women, what in fact happened was invocation of Muslim women as 'mothers, sisters and daughters' before all else. One particularly public example of this was the 'Making a Stand' campaign spearheaded by the now defunct 'women's led counter-extremism organisation, Inspire'.[34] Inspire operated according to the Prevent paradigm, which upheld that the barriers facing Muslim women's progress were to be located within Muslim communities and that Muslim women are therefore potential agents in combatting extremism. Inspire counter-extremism initiatives sought to empower Muslim women to challenge the extremism 'within their communities'.[35] This included training women to spot the signs of radicalisation in their children so they could 'safeguard against extremism'.[36] Making a Stand was a government-funded project that launched in the *Sun* newspaper with a front page depicting a brown woman adorned in a Union Jack headscarf.[37] The campaign was a response to the formation of the Islamic State, which saw young Muslims from Britain and elsewhere in Europe leaving to join the group.

The Inspire campaign consisted of a series of brightly-lit videos accompanied by uplifting music and opening with the Inspire logo adorned with a butterfly. A sequence of women appear – often in hijab though sometimes without – to speak about their participation in the campaign. Each video concludes with a participant holding up a placard with the hashtag #MakingAStand, the music reaches a crescendo and the words 'My name is [...] and I'm making a stand' are spoken. Making a Stand is thereby firmly embedded within the logics of Prevent, including upholding the collective responsibility of Muslims for terrorist violence and locating the causes of radicalisation within Muslim communities. For example, one participant speaks about how upset she is at 'such a high number of our youngsters' joining IS and underlines her personal responsibility in tackling this.[38] Another participant talks about how illiteracy among older Muslims has caused a generational rift with young people navigating life in Britain.[39]

However, the participants are not only seeking to challenge the threat of extremism, but they link this effort to the fight for gender equality. One participant talks about the importance of Muslim women speaking out because it is 'men who are usually talking and their voices are being heard.'[40] Another claims that going back into her community to help 'mums' and 'youngsters' is also 'empowering women' because 'we have rights and we should fight for them.'[41] However, what all participants stress in different ways is their identity as *British* Muslim women. One participant talks about focusing on 'the plus side of being British' because in some countries you are not able to practise your faith freely.'[42] Someone else speaks about how 'bringing up children in this country is obviously a great thing. I mean I was brought up in this country.'[43] Collectively, the videos suggest that being a 'good Muslim' means living like you are 'British' and Muslims should open their eyes to the manifold opportunities of living in Britain.

At the campaign's launch, the then home secretary Theresa May said, 'I truly believe that as women, as mothers, sisters and daughters you have a unique and powerful role to play in helping to combat the extremist challenge here and abroad.'[44] While challenging the threat of extremism is presented as a vehicle for gender equality, the assumptions which underpin this argument are ultimately racist and patriarchal. Firstly, the notion that women are well placed to challenge their extremist men folk rests on their roles as 'mothers, sisters and daughters'. In other words, Muslim women are here defined in relation to the men in their lives and not as agents in themselves – a strange sort of gender equality. There are also echoes here of colonial wars of pacification such as the Algerian War of Independence. The French colonisers felt Muslim women could be mobilised to pacify Algerian men and, in the process, liberate themselves. So-called 'unveiling ceremonies' were carried out by 'the wives of French military officers who unveiled some Algerian women to show that they were now siding with their French "sisters".'[45] These efforts glossed over the fact that Algerian Muslim women were also part of a violent anti-colonial independence movement.

Secondly, the idea that women are somehow inherently more 'peaceful' is another outdated gendered trope which denies Muslim women the kind of full political agency – the ability to act politically – available to men. This does not only relate to the issue of the use of political violence but to the idea that women cannot be engaged in political struggle to contest, challenge or change things and that they believe might need changing. Instead, women are cast as pliable, peaceable and accommodating figures who can be invoked, mobilised and cast as the useful handmaidens of state power. The figure of the Muslim woman adorned in a Union Jack headscarf, which made the *Sun*'s front cover, could also be seen in other iterations, including on the 'Making a Stand' literature visible in the videos. This image should not be seen as the model for an 'empowered' Muslim woman. It should be seen for what is actually is: an attempt to inscribe the values of a racist and colonially inflected British state upon the very bodies of Muslim women.

### Muslim children

The impact of Prevent on the lives of Muslim children comes into occasional, if partial, focus through headlines such as 'Muslim boy, 4, was referred to Prevent over game of *Fortnite*'[46] and 'Nursery raised fears of radicalisation over boy's cucumber drawing'.[47] What often gets passed over in these eyecatching headlines is the impact on the children and families concerned. One eleven-year-old boy was referred to Prevent for saying he wanted to give 'alms to the oppressed' which was misheard by his teacher as 'arms'.[48] In the Prevent referral notes the boy is regarded as having an 'atypical' interest in 'mediaeval history, war, siege engines and soldiers' and as attending 'the local mosque'.[49] While the case was dismissed by police, the Prevent referral remains on the record of the child and goes with him throughout his future schooling. In fact, all Prevent referrals can be found on the National Police Prevent Case Management (PCM), a secret database that was uncovered by the human rights organisation Liberty. The database includes children, and anyone with a Prevent referral can find themselves on it irrespective of whether their case was escalated to a Channel panel.[50] In other words, you do not have to be convicted of anything, be guilty of any crime, or even be suspected of exhibiting radical views to end up on the database.

This discussion underlines that Muslim children are not exempt from the violent machinery of Prevent by virtue of being children. Children are in fact the captive audience of Prevent, who are taught British values from nursery to the end of their formal education and are continually monitored for signs of radicalisation by their teachers. 'Misheard' phrases which are made possible through framing of Muslim populations as threatening to Britishness have turned the lives of unsuspected children and their families upside down. Muslim children are therefore just as much part of the pact of collective responsibility for terrorism and radicalisation that was handed to Muslim communities in the wake of 9/11 and 7/7. They are not presumed to be innocent, but are burdened with the inheritance of their Muslimness, which like adults renders them always potentially threatening.[51] Therefore, the ways in which the citizenship of Muslims is made conditional, and their ability to act politically is forestalled, begins in childhood.

Western notions of 'inheritance' are very much tied to the accumulation of various kinds of property that you pass on to your offspring. This is why inheritance tax is seen as a moral evil by the political right in Britain, because it is perceived as the theft of earned entitlements. However, there are also accumulations of a different kind which have little to do with the transmission of wealth but the passing down of histories and attributes which render the citizenship of Muslim children conditional. An instructive example can be found in the United States where scholars have explored the idea that Black children are not regarded as 'innocent' or even as 'children' in the way that white children are. Phillip Atiba Goff et al found that Black boys are perceived as less 'childlike' than white boys and dehumanized through racial stereotypes including 'associating them (implicitly) with apes'.[52] Black boys are also rendered as legitimate targets for police violence because they are seen as being responsible for their actions just like adults.

Similarly, the term 'adultification' captures the way Black girls in schools are seen as more adult and less innocent than their white counterparts. This can lead to harsher punishments within schools and within the juvenile justice system.[53] The lack of innocence afforded to Black children has been traced to histories of chattel slavery in the United States, where children were not excluded from the regimes of human being owned as property.[54] The racist and dehumanising tropes which applied to Black adults also awaited Black children, and this inheritance continues to fuel the contemporary violence they face.

This inheritance, that of being from 'somewhere else', is held by legions of British citizens who hail from Commonwealth states such as Jamaica, Pakistan, India and Nigeria. It is worth noting that this 'somewhere else' does not include white settler states of the Commonwealth which feel familiar, closer and where immigration to and from these spaces has historically been comparatively easy and seen as a desirable thing. The most extreme consequence of this inheritance for Muslim children can be seen in the abandonment of Shamima Begum and her children. She was a child when she left for Syria and her three children who were all British citizens also died in al-Roj camp. According to Save the Children, over 60 British children remain in Syrian camps and only those who have been orphaned have the option of repatriation.[55]

Despite the fact that these Muslim children had nothing to do with the choices of their parents – they cannot share in any of the decision making or responsibility regarding where they ended up – they have been effectively abandoned by the state. While Britain offered to repatriate orphaned or unaccompanied children, for those that had parents family separation was the only way back. States like Germany and Denmark repatriated women and children from camps characterised as 'violent, unsanitary and inhumane' because 'the children are not responsible for their situation' but Britain remains an outlier in its approach.[56] Despite being 'innocent victims of conflict' the state appears to have no interest in the welfare of these Muslim children despite their citizenship status. What does this example tell us about the wider relationship between the British state and its Muslim citizens? That the formal legal status of British citizen offers no protection against either harm or death and nor does being a child.

Ultimately, the fate of these abandoned children is tied to the fate of their counterparts residing in Britain where arguably all that separates them is the Prevent strategy. Muslim children have inherited the guilt of collective responsibility that was conferred on their elders and are thereby not presumed to be innocent. In 2015, the Bureau of Investigative Journalism found that three schools in Barnsley – an area where far-right activity from groups like the EDL and BNP has been historically high – claimed 'that white pupils are at low risk of radicalisation on account of their skin colour and because many families have links to the Armed Forces'.[57] While Black and Asian students in the schools were being monitored, white students were deemed 'low risk'. Muslim children have been accused of holding 'terrorist-like views' for supporting the Boycott, Divestment and Sanctions campaign aimed at the state of Israel and for being referred to Social Service for using the term 'Allah Akbar' (God is great).[58] Therefore, the cases of nurseries and schools reporting young children for supposedly exhibiting signs of radicalisation should not surprise us, because these seemingly shocking instances are actually part of the wider pattern of policing of Muslim children through Prevent.

Another impact of this policing has been what scholars call the 'chilling effect' or self-censorship in which Muslim children engage, in order not to draw unwanted attention. A great deal of attention has been focused on Muslim students at university who are forced into censoring their views and modifying their behaviour in order to avoid being labelled an extremist, but similar trends can also be found in schools. Academics at Middlesex University found that the Prevent Duty 'disproportionately impacted' Muslim children who felt stigmatised and under scrutiny.[59] This trend relates to the adoption of British Values which makes some children feel like their Muslimness is a marker of extremism.[60] As I explored in the previous chapter, British Values are racially coded and foreground an idea of a white Britain threatened by Muslim citizens. These values function both as pedagogical tools to teach children about acceptable British conduct and also as a tool of surveillance shedding light on those considered to be potential extremists. This means Muslim children are often marked as already threatening prior even to the enactment of the Prevent Duty and teaching of British Values in classrooms.

# 4

# *The Hostile Environment*

In Britain, the most brutal, and wide-ranging racism which occurs day after day is not the work of fascist minority parties but of Her Majesty's government. It is the racism written into, and demanded by Britain's immigration rules.

Amrit Wilson[1]

During the first Covid-19 lockdown in Britain, Brexit Party leader Nigel Farage was visited by police for breaking restriction rules. It transpired that in early 2020, Farage had travelled over 100 miles to Dover in order to report on the 'migrant scandal' of people crossing the English Channel in order to come to Britain.[2] Over the course of the pandemic, the sight of vulnerable people huddled on inflatable dinghies created new and valuable political opportunities for Britain's government to show it was tough on immigration. Home secretary Priti Patel sought to enlist the Royal Navy in helping to push back boats to France and the Royal National Lifeboat Institution (RNLI), which carries out search and rescue operations, was branded as a 'migrant taxi service'.[3] The deaths of people forced to make unsafe crossings are invariably described as a 'tragedies' with people smugglers being held accountable as the chief perpetrators.[4]

In reality, successive pieces of British immigration legislation are responsible for criminalising the freedom of movement that make safe passage without assistance from smugglers impossible. The ramping up of punitive measures against people on the move to Britain is no accident, but forms part of a deliberately constructed hostile environment which is designed to make life unliveable for the popularly reviled 'illegal immigrant'. The Nationality and Borders Bill currently making its way through the legislative process has been recognised by the United Nations High Commissioner for Refugees (UNHCR) as undermining the rights of asylum seekers enshrined in international law. Key provisions in the bill mean the further criminalisation of those seeking refuge in Britain and the power to push back asylum seekers arriving by boat. Even the 'Homes for Ukraine' scheme launched by the British government in response to public sympathy for refugees fleeing a Russian invasion has been slow in responding to the demand for entry to Britain. We cannot understand this current push to reduce the basic rights of refugees without first considering the crucial role of the hostile environment legislation which preceded it.

While Theresa May argued that the hostile environment was directed at undocumented migrants, it has had a devastating impact on Britain's postcolonial citizens by calling into question their belonging. This chapter explores how we can think about the hostile environment as a set of immigration controls embedded in the everyday where citizens have to provide proof of entitlement before they can access employment, healthcare or welfare. Through the hostile environment, Britain's postcolonial citizens who were not white and considered to be less 'British' came into the purview of state border violence. The Windrush scandal showed how immigration legislation aimed at keeping out non-citizens led to thousands of Black and brown Britons losing their jobs, homes, benefits, access to healthcare and in some cases being deported. The hostile environment, like the Prevent Strategy before it, has effectively instituted a more formalised regime of everyday racial bordering making the citizenship of Britain's postcolonial people conditional.

The build-up to the hostile environment enacted through the Immigration Acts 2014 and 2016 was a long time in the making. In the last twenty years we have seen the mainstreaming of historically far right views and demands for controls on immigration by all major political parties. In her investigation of the Windrush scandal, Wendy Williams showed that New Labour's immigration and asylum policies presaged the hostile environment. From making it harder to apply for asylum status or citizenship to denying access to welfare provisions for applicants through No Recourse to Public Funds (NRPF), to overseeing the establishment of immigration detention centres. Maya Goodfellow also argues, however, that in the early 2000s a popular narrative had been disseminated of the New Labour government as an out-of-touch government permissive on immigration.[5] In response, New Labour adopted increasingly draconian rhetoric and measures on 'illegal' immigrants, 'bogus' asylum seekers and refugees.

Since the Second World War, discourses on immigration have centred on the idea of a liberal elite set of politicians betraying what should be their most important constituency: white British voters. This most recent 'betrayal' of white British voters was founded on figures which showed that between 1993 and 2011, there was a rise in 'the number of people in the UK who were born abroad' from 3.8 million to 7 million.[6] New Labour's time in office also coincided with the enlargement of the European Union in 2004, which saw the arrival of over a million EU nationals to Britain, as well as a rise in asylum seekers from conflict areas such as Kosovo and Afghanistan. Goodfellow argues it is not the immigration numbers which are intrinsically problematic, but the meaning that has come to be attached to them.[7] This meaning was tied to the ideas of who should (and should not) be able to enter Britain and who should (or should not) be entitled to access employment, housing, healthcare, education and welfare benefits. Media-led moral panics surrounding so-called 'health tourism' and migrant 'benefit scroungers' abounded at this time, dominating both tabloid and broadsheet newspapers.

The 2010 election of the Conservative-led coalition government signalled the expansion and intensification of Britain's anti-immigration policies. Elected on a promise of cutting overall net migration to 'the tens of thousands', the Conservative Party signalled its intent early on.[8] In 2013, the Home Office launched Operation Vaken, where they deployed 'Go Home' vans to drive around 'six of the most ethnically diverse London boroughs'.[9] The vans read 'in the UK illegally? Go home or face arrest'. Hannah Jones et al point out that, 'the moment of the Go Home van seemed to us to be a turning point in the climate of immigration debates – a ratcheting up of anti-migrant feeling to the point where it was possible for a government-sponsored advertisement to use the same hate speech and rhetoric as far-right racists.'[10]

This chapter maps the emergence of the hostile environment from a ministerial working group to an enacted piece of legislation. I set out how this policy agenda formed in the context of the increasing prominence of UKIP, a party once described by David Cameron as 'swivel-eyed loons' but who came to mainstream with what were once extreme positions on immigration. These positions were taken up with increasing alacrity by all three mainstream political parties in Britain. Therefore, the architecture of the hostile environment and the ideas which underpin it implicate an entire political class and not just a few bad apples. For Britain's postcolonial citizens, these changes in immigration law would mean the formal borders of the nation were no longer to be experienced at airports or embassies but would become part of the fabric of their everyday lives.

## What is the hostile environment?

The 'hostile environment' is an umbrella term for a set of immigration controls embedded in the institutions of everyday life. These controls make life in Britain unliveable for those without the paperwork to prove their entitlements to access public goods, housing, and employment and banking services. This legislation has fundamentally altered the relationship between the state and its citizens, requiring the latter to assume the responsibility of providing proof of entitlement to access public goods such as education or healthcare. While theoretically these immigration controls have implications for *every* British citizen, they are particularly concerning for Britain's postcolonial citizens. These immigration controls were brought into law despite criticisms that they would lead to discrimination against Britain's postcolonial citizens whose belonging in white Britain would not be assumed. Nonetheless May vigorously defended the hostile environment, describing it as a corrective to an unfair system in which those with 'no right to be here in the UK' were able to 'exist as everybody else does with bank accounts, with driving licences and with access to rented accommodation.'[11]

The controls were introduced through the Immigration Acts of 2014 and 2016 and require individuals to provide proof of their immigration status in order to access work, healthcare, education, banking, driving and welfare benefits. These border checks span across the public and private sector, engaging multiple institutions and actors including schools, colleges, universities, employers, landlords, the DVLA and banks. Failure to undertake checks can result in fines for landlords and employers. Sitting alongside border checks are a wider web of policing practices which include immigration raids, detention and deportation targeted at those who cannot provide evidence of their immigration status. Finally, the Home Office is also building what it calls the Status Checking Database containing the immigration status of migrants in order to facilitate data sharing between the government and different agencies involved in border work.

This book does not focus on how the hostile environment has impacted on non-citizens – the people at who it was ostensibly aimed – such as undocumented migrants, asylum seekers and refugees. However, it is written from the understanding that violence directed at those designated as outsiders to white Britain happens on a continuum. In other words, Prevent and the hostile environment show that those racialised as non-white can never be safe in their belonging in Britain – whether or not they are citizens. After all, the Immigration Acts of 2014 and 2016 turned members of the Windrush generation into undocumented migrants despite their having arrived in Britain through regularised routes as citizens. However, citizenship offers an additional layer of protection which is not accessible to Black and brown non-citizens.

Histories of immigration law, nationality law and asylum law in Britain show that these policy agendas developed in response to white anxieties about the movement of colonial subjects to the metropole.[12] These overlapping areas of legislation have centred on upholding white entitlement and determining who is and is not a citizen at any given time. Legislation aimed at managing different types of migration reflects the national compact which charged Britain's political classes with the task of prioritising the rights and entitlements of white Britons to welfare and public services over those of their postcolonial cousins.

It is unsurprising that the Conservative Party's 2010 general election manifesto commitment to introduce a 'fairer' immigration system targeting undocumented migrants, also came with a promise to reduce the overall net migration of *documented* migrants. In other words, these were postcolonial citizens who, historically, have had the legal right to come to Britain but whose rights have been hacked away by decades of racist immigration legislation.

It is also important to understand that the racism experienced by postcolonial citizens is itself not a new situation nor are the barriers they face in accessing public goods as part of their rights and entitlements. Racialized immigration practices and the existence of a colour bar which has limited the ability of postcolonial citizens to access labour markets, housing, welfare and other public services have long histories in post-war Britain.[13] However, the hostile environment signals both a qualitative and quantitative shift in how racial violence is structured and meted out by the state and experienced by postcolonial citizens. The Immigration Acts of 2014 and 2016 have formalised through the law the connection between immigration status and the entitlement to access public goods.

This legislation represents the systematic entrenchment of border controls into everyday life which impact on postcolonial citizens because they are not considered to be unconditionally 'British'. As a result, this legislation has led to an increase in spaces where postcolonial citizens experience racism as part of their everyday lives. Border checks which span the institutions of everyday life feed into an atmosphere of mistrust between ordinary people and their doctors, educators and employers. Campaign groups like 'Docs not Cops', 'Against Borders for Children' and 'Unis Resist Border Controls' are documenting and resisting the harmful impact of the hostile environment in healthcare, schools and universities.

As the ongoing Windrush scandal shows, people who arrived in Britain as Commonwealth subjects were asked to provide proof of their immigration status before being able to access public goods. When they could not, they lost jobs, were prevented from accessing welfare benefits, were denied life-saving healthcare, and became subject to detention and deportation. As Armağan Teke Lloyd argues, 'Migration management represents a global "carceral archipelago" in Foucault's terms . . . wherein immigrants are policed by gates, walls, oceans, surveillance cameras, checkpoints and background clearances'.[14] Global immigration controls have become inescapable for those who are on the move precisely because they are embedded in everyday life as mundane and bureaucratic processes. The border is no longer at the airport, it is everywhere.

### The hostile environment: a cross-party consensus

Anti-immigration politics are a prominent feature of postcolonial Britain, yet the provenance of the hostile environment lies in the more recent discontent surrounding developments under the New Labour government. The expansion of the EU in 2004 marked a significant moment in the intensification of violent rhetoric about 'swarms' and 'floods' of migrants arriving to displace the rights and entitlements of white Britons, to work and public services. At this time a consensus emerged across political divides which was shared by all three major parties that *something must be done* about Britain's immigration system. This convergence led to the mainstreaming of extreme positions on immigration which had been held by relatively marginal far-right parties like the BNP and UKIP during the 1990s and early 2000s.

When the Conservative-led coalition government came to power in 2010 they did so following a campaign which focused on their commitment to reducing overall net migration, placing them closer to what, only five years previously, had been considered to be an extremist position expounded by the likes of the BNP. Moreover, the promise to introduce a restrictive Australian-style points-based system which would allow higher earning 'skilled migrants' to enter the country was not dissimilar to the position of the outgoing New Labour government or of current Labour leader, Keir Starmer. This was a way of keeping out those on lower incomes who overwhelmingly tend to be subjects of the new Commonwealth such as Pakistan, Bangladesh, India and Nigeria.

Under Gordon Brown's leadership, New Labour signalled it was in favour of introducing a more restrictive system, with the key difference being that unlike the Conservatives they would not place a cap on overall numbers migrating to Britain. In fact, prior to the 'election' in 2007, in the face of criticism from across the political spectrum that the Labour Party had abandoned their own 'traditional' constituency of (white) working class voters because its commitment to globalisation and freedom of movement, leading Brown to promise 'British jobs for British workers'.

This view was cemented in the 2010 General Election when Brown was heckled by a 65-year-old pensioner Gillian Duffy during a campaign speech in Rochdale. At the behest of his advisor, Brown spoke with Duffy who said, 'You can't say anything about the immigrants because you're saying that you're [...] but all these eastern European what are coming in, where are they flocking from?'[15] At the end of the exchange Brown was heard calling Duffy, who had also expressed concerns about Labour's welfare reform and tuition fees, 'that bigoted woman.'[16] This moment led to a national scandal in which New Labour was painted as out of touch with its (white) working class voters.

In this increasingly nativist context, Nigel Farage's leadership of the anti-EU and anti-immigration UKIP Party represented both a symbolic and electoral challenge to the Conservatives and Labour. By this time Gillian Duffy had been cynically cast by the media and politicians in the role of the barometer for the views of the white working class. In an interview with the *Telegraph* she noted Farage's pint-drinking persona represented his authenticity and an ability to connect with white voters supposedly sneered upon by Labour elites. Despite being a wealthy former city banker, Farage was considered to be relatable to the working-class Duffy precisely because of his unabashed 'honesty' about immigration.

The 2010 General Election sounded the alarm bells for both Labour and the Conservatives due to UKIP's ability to appeal to white voters from across the political spectrum. The outcome of a hung parliament led some to conclude a Conservative majority had been squeezed by UKIP, despite the fact UKIP only obtained 3% of the national vote share. UKIP, once branded as a party of 'fruitcakes and loonies and closet racists' by Cameron, was however central to shifting the Overton window on what could be said by more mainstream politicians and political parties about immigration. Saying the supposedly unsayable, a role once played by Enoch Powell – for whom Farage has expressed a deep affinity – was precisely what white voters like Duffy admired about the 'straight talking' Farage. Crucially, his narratives about immigration, the EU and the supplanting of British sovereignty were adopted by all the major parties.

Amelia Gentleman argues that Theresa May's speech at the Conservative Party conference in 2011 reflected this tendency. Gentleman writes, 'May poured scorn on the human rights-based appeals that she believed were complicating the deportation process, claiming that in one case an illegal immigrant could not be deported "because – and I'm not making this up – he had a pet cat".'[17] Unfortunately, May *was* making it up. It transpired that this story had initially been shared by Nigel Farage but was later debunked by the Royal Courts of Justice after May's speech. Hostility towards the Human Rights Act (HRA) within the Conservative Party and in right-wing newspapers dated back to 2004, when the New Labour govenmernt introduced the HRA by incorporating the European Convention on Human Rights (ECHR) into domestic British law. The legislation proved controversial because the HRA was seen as supplanting British parliamentary sovereignty in key policy areas such as criminal justice, immigration, counter-terrorism and even planning laws. In 2022, the ECHR grounded the first flight seeking to deport asylum seekers from Britain to Rwanda, reviving hostility towards the HRA and ECHR.

Human rights-based challenges to immigration rulings and counter-terrorism measures have always proved especially controversial. Shortly after the HRA was passed into law, then Conservative Party leader Michael Howard argued he would scrap the legislation should his party form the next government on the basis it was 'politically correct', invited litigious behaviour and undermined 'British traditions of fairness'.[18] Over time opposition towards the HRA crystallised at the intersection of broader anti-European sentiment, Islamophobia and a broader xenophobia targeted at migrants. Critics of the HRA argued that Britain's borders could not be effectively protected from criminals and terrorists within, or immigrants without because the British government had to obey rules made by that infamous bogeyman: the faceless Brussels bureaucrat. This is despite the fact the HRA is part of international law and adjudicated by the European Court of Human Rights (ECHR) which is not part of the EU.

Once again, actual facts did not deter the Conservative Party from tying the issue of EU membership to the battle for reducing immigration numbers and combating terrorism in defence of Britain's borders. In fact, these tropes became a recurrent feature of May's speeches. May's speech at the party conference in 2012 demonstrated how the Conservatives were central to mainstreaming rhetoric that had once been the preserve of the once marginal UKIP. May opened her speech by rhetorically asking, 'Wasn't it great to say goodbye – at long last – to Abu Hamza and those four other terror suspects on Friday?'[19] Abu Hamza Al-Masri, an Egyptian national, regularly described as a 'preacher of hate' was also central to the controversy surrounding Finsbury Park Mosque. He had been questioned by Scotland Yard in relation to alleged bomb plots in Yemen, but was later convicted in 2006 for inciting murder and race hate.

After an extradition request from the US for Abu Hamza, his legal representation took the case and that of the other four men to the ECHR. They argued that the human rights of the subjects would be violated if they stood trial in the US. While the ECHR had initially blocked extradition attempts, it later ruled that the men could in fact be tried in the US. But this outcome did little to stem the tide of anger directed toward the HRA. In the 2015 General Election, the Conservative Party was promising a British Bill of Rights (BBR) which would 'break the formal link between British courts and the European Court of Human Rights, and make our own Supreme Court the ultimate arbiter of human rights matters in the UK'.[20] Arguing in support of a BBR, Allison Pearson claimed 'The dreadful Human Rights Act has actually made the people of Britain less safe, because it has weakened our ability to expel those who mean us harm'.[21]

The *Daily Mail* described the Conservatives' promise as 'an end of the human rights farce' through which Britain could 'ignore the European Court and its crazy decisions.'[22] Migrants, terrorists and Gypsy, Roma and Traveller communities – who were all presented as being beneficiaries of the HRA and seen as exploiting its right to family life as well as claiming welfare benefits – could all expect 'fairer' treatment through the BBR. Connecting immigration, terrorism and welfare to the protection of British borders is premised on the idea that national resources belong to deserving (white) Britons. Detractors of the HRA fervently argued that this treaty prevented the British government from exercising sovereignty within its own borders. Debates about sovereignty were also connected to membership of the EU, where freedom of movement was seen as getting in the way of cutting overall net migration. It is in this context that the push to create an ever more hostile environment for all migrants took shape. From this perspective the idea of 'taking back control' of Britain's borders, a slogan coined by the Vote Leave campaign in 2016, was well underway prior to the referendum.

*From a ministerial working group to legislation*

In 2012, the Hostile Environment ministerial working group was established two years into the Coalition government, amidst concerns that the Conservatives would not be able to deliver on their promise to cut net migration. The working group was created with the express purpose 'of requiring ministers across government to come up with new ways to make immigrants' lives more difficult, by outsourcing the scrutiny of their legal status to professionals who must act as unpaid immigration officers.'[23] It was later renamed as 'The Inter-Ministerial Group on Migrants' Access to Benefits and Public Services' (MATBAPS), at the behest of the Conservative's queasy but obliging coalition partners, the Liberal Democrats.[24] However, despite the change in name, the function of MATBAPS remained to ensure access to public services, housing, employment, education and welfare would be impossible without papers.

While some argued that the Liberal Democrats acted as a break on the Conservative Party's worst instincts, MP Sarah Teather cited 'a consensus among the three party leaders' about immigration.[25] Agreement centred on the issue of 'illegal immigrants', whereby the Liberal Democrats were largely in alignment with their Conservative partners that Britain's immigration system needed to be more robust. David Laws, a Liberal Democrat cabinet minister, worked with Conservative MP Oliver Letwin to demand a 'Border systems stock take' to account for people entering and leaving the UK. When told by senior civil servant Bob Kerslake that immigration was not a priority for the Home Office like crime or terrorism, Laws wrote, 'This is all extraordinary. No wonder there is little public confidence in the immigration system.'[26] Laws also described Home Secretary Theresa May as having 'a tough reputation on immigration' but 'going after the easiest targets, which aren't the real problem.'[27]

Any disagreements within the Coalition government about the hostile environment were focused on how far-reaching policies would be, as opposed to whether they were necessary let alone ethical. MATBAPS was formed of ministers and senior civil servants from across a range of key policy areas which included work, welfare, health, education and housing. Laws notes the progress and tension within one particular MATBAPS meeting: 'IDS [Iain Duncan Smith] started on benefits, which went perfectly well. Jeremy Hunt then made quite a good pitch on health. We then went on to private landlords, where the Prime Minister quite frankly wants to go much further than Eric Pickles.'[28] The banality of tone sits in stark contrast with the issues that were being discussed: namely making the lives of undocumented people in Britain unliveable by denying them access to the basic necessities of life.

A well-documented moment of tension arose at this meeting between Cameron and Pickles, the latter serving in the cabinet as Communities Secretary. Pickles argued against immigration checks being conducted by 'smaller private landlords' because this may lead to discrimination against anyone 'foreign' or 'foreign-looking.'[29] Vince Cable also made a 'blunt contribution' in which he argued that 'prejudiced twaddle about immigration' should be dismissed on the doorstep.[30] According to Laws, no-one supported the Prime Minister's position on landlords aside from Oliver Letwin, prompting Cameron to bring the meeting to

THE VIOLENCE OF BRITISHNESS

an abrupt end and walk out. In spite of these tensions every single MP – Conservative and Liberal Democrat – present in this meeting voted for the resultant Immigration Bill 2014. In so doing they brought into effect some of the most extensive and intrusive border checks in British history. Out of the 311 MPs who attended the vote in parliament, only 16 voted against the bill including Jeremy Corbyn and Diane Abbott.

Then Labour Party leader Ed Miliband advised his MPs to abstain from the vote altogether. Shadow Home Secretary Yvette Cooper argued the Immigration Act 2014 'contained some "sensible" ideas but offered "nothing" to ensure immigrants would not be used to undercut wages'.[31] In a *Guardian* article in which Cooper wrote about addressing public anxiety over immigration she noted, 'Low-paid workers see deep injustice in the way employers exploit cheap migrant labour to undercut wages. Communities are worried about public services as budgets are cut'.[32] The Migration Observatory has described the impact of migration on the employment of UK-born workers to be non-existent or small and the impact of migration on wages to be 'small'.[33] However, blaming migrants for driving down wages without a view to the evidence enabled an alignment between the Labour Party and its (white) working class voter's concerns on immigration. Indeed, the question of migration, jobs and wages is an old one on the British left, one reflected in the histories of British labour movements divided by these issues.[34]

Nor did the Labour Party challenge the argument that migrants place pressure on public services, the biggest threat to which was actually the Coalition government's austerity cuts, which saw local government budgets cut by up to 50% over ten years.[35] This period of austerity saw the closure of key public services in many areas, including women's shelters, youth provisions and homeless services.[36] This was in addition to the overall reduction in central government spending on health and education.[37] Cooper amplified rather than challenged key untruths about immigration that were being wielded by the far-right and mainstreamed by the Conservatives. This position allowed Labour to present their anti-immigration stance as progressive by comparison because it was fundamentally concerned with worker exploitation, worker's rights and a concern for the preservation of public services.

It was clear from both Miliband's injunction to Labour MPs to abstain from the vote and Cooper's criticisms of the Immigration Bill, that since being ejected from office in 2010, the Labour Party were keen to rebrand themselves as a party that understood the concerns of white British voters. In the 2015 general election, Labour's now infamous 'Controls on Immigration' mug was sold as party merchandise to draw voter attention to their 'tough' policies. This included a ban on EU nationals claiming welfare benefits for two years after their arrival as well as a ban on sending child benefits abroad. Miliband also frequently attacked the Conservative Party for not meeting their target of reducing net migration and pointed to the number of people entering the country as an example of 'broken promises'.[38]

However, as Stephen Bush noted at the time, this lurch to the right on immigration did little for Labour's electoral prospects. As he wrote, 'Increasingly rancorous language about migrants and benefits has done nothing to secure Labour's increasingly alarming position in the polls'.[39] The Conservative Party's 12 seat majority at the 2015 General Election confirmed the idea that Labour was simply not convincing anyone of its anti-immigration position. Laws noted in a somewhat scathing fashion, 'We agreed that Ed Miliband was a nice guy but not a very convincing Prime Minister – his heart is really on the soggy left of British politics, so when he makes speeches about welfare scroungers or immigration, it just doesn't have any credibility'.[40]

It has become commonplace to regard the Conservative Party as uniquely responsible for the ills in British politics and in particular for the toxic rhetoric surrounding the issue of immigration. However, the pantomime villain status of being the 'nasty party' from which the Conservatives have benefited handsomely at recent general elections serves a more insidious and overlooked function in British politics. Namely, it draws attention away from the emergent consensus *across the political spectrum* regarding the need to reform a 'chaotic' immigration system and about the undesirability of immigrants themselves, whether they are designated as regular or irregular depending on how the lines have shifted beneath their feet.

Anti-immigration views in fact cut across all three major parties, spanning from the far-right, across the left/liberal centre, to also be found among some of the white left of 'blue' Labour. Without its Liberal Democrat partners and an acquiescent Labour Party, the Conservatives would not have been able to pass such far reaching legislation through parliament. From this perspective every appalling detail about the Windrush scandal which has come to light in the last few years is not simply an indictment of figures such as David Cameron, Theresa May and Amber Rudd. The Windrush scandal must be remembered as a symptom of something considerably graver: namely the profound failure of an entire political class that was fully complicit in the violence perpetrated against Britain's postcolonial citizens in the name of whiteness.

## Immigration Acts 2014 and 2016

In this section, I outline three key aspects of the Immigration Acts 2014 and 2016 and how this legislation entrenched border checks into everyday life. These are the 'Right to Rent', the 'Right to Work' and the Home Office's database, the Status Verification and Enquiries Checking (SVEC) for accessing the NHS. These immigration controls effectively outsource border control to employers of public sector workers like doctors and teachers and to private individuals such as landlords. The hostile environment is made possible by data sharing between government departments, the private sector and immigration enforcement. Once you have 'failed' an immigration check such as Right to Rent or Right to Work, this is recorded and shared between different actors undertaking immigration enforcement. These measures operate alongside an expansion of policing powers which constitute what Teke Lloyd described as the inescapable 'carceral archipelago' which encompasses immigration raids, detention and deportation to which individuals are subjected if they do not pass these checks.

While the hostile environment includes immigration controls in the areas of education, banking and driving, this chapter focuses on housing, work and healthcare to underline how access to basic needs is being denied to Britain's postcolonial citizens. However, it is important to acknowledge that being unable to access banking and driving makes it impossible for citizens to carry out everyday tasks such as paying rent, paying for mobile phone contracts or being able to freely move around.[41] The civil rights think tank Liberty has argued that denying undocumented migrants the right to drive will also increase police stop and searches, which are already controversial given they are overwhelmingly targeted at Black and Asian people.[42]

## Right to Rent

Right to rent (RtR) checks were introduced through the Immigration Act 2014 as a series of pilot programmes ostensibly subject to evaluation to check for their efficacy and potentially discriminatory effects. RtR was rolled out on a national basis through the Immigration Act 2016, alongside new policing powers in which landlords who knowingly rented to individuals without requisite paperwork could be imprisoned for up to five years and levied with a fine. Prior to the pilot programmes, and up to their national implementation across England, the racially discriminatory implications of RtR were being flagged up for the attention of the Home Office.[43] The response of the Home Office was to ensure that landlords would self-regulate through a 'non-discrimination code' with no oversight or enforcement of this.[44] These concerns were again raised in parliament during the committee stage of the Immigration Bill. Furthermore, the issue of British citizens without requisite paperwork who would find it difficult to rent private accommodation was also raised at this time but these concerns were brushed aside. This reality was reflected in both the evaluation of the pilot programmes and in national implementation. RtR was designed to do the following four things:

1. Make it more difficult for illegally resident individuals to gain access to privately rented accommodation, and so deter those who are illegally resident from remaining in the UK;
2. deter those who seek to exploit illegal residents by providing illegal and unsafe accommodation, and increase actions against them;

3. deter individuals from attempting to enter the UK illegally, and undermine the market for those who seek to facilitate illegal migration or traffic migrant workers;

4. tackle rogue landlords by increasing joint working between the Home Office, local authorities and other government departments.[45]

RtR was initially trialled for six months in parts of Birmingham, Dudley, Walsall, Sandwell and Wolverhampton. The Home Office provided no rationale for the choice of location for these pilots but the Joint Council for the Welfare of Immigrants (JCWI) noted the absence of London boroughs from the impact evaluation would give only a partial picture of the impact of RtR.[46] This was because the pilot could not 'foresee the more considerable impacts in a high pressure rental market such as London, where the UK's migrant population is also concentrated.'[47] However, the Home Office's evaluation found that Black and Asian people were asked to provide more information during rental enquiries that white British people.[48] This view was reinforced by David Bolt, the Independent Chief Inspector of Borders and Immigration, who found 'The policy has resulted in instances of discrimination against tenants, including BME tenants, who do have the Right to Rent in the UK.'[49]

The JCWI also found that 'As a direct result of the Right to Rent scheme, landlords are now less likely to rent to people without a British passport, those with foreign accents or people who have a name which doesn't sound British.'[50] Earlier in 2017, JCWI had also found 'tenants had been wrongly refused tenancies owing to confusion among landlords and there were a number of worrying reports of harassment by landlords.'[51] The Legal Action Group also reported on 'surprised Brits' who were finding their lack of a British passport was making it impossible for them to rent accommodation, find employment and access welfare benefits.[52] LAG's interviews with surprised Brits showed how they were caught by surprise at the legislative changes, which required them to flourish a passport that might never have existed or was long since lost and not replaced.

Ultimately, the Home Office evaluation chose not to engage meaningfully with RtR's racially discriminatory implications. Despite the extent of concerns raised about RtR it was rolled out across England prior to the publication of the problematic Home Office's evaluation. Nor was there any mechanism through which tenants could report or appeal against what they considered to discriminatory outcomes of RtR checks. The Immigration Act 2016 strengthened punitive powers compelling landlords to undertake immigration checks through the introduction of a criminal offence for renting to those without paperwork proving entitlement in addition to fines. In 2018, the JCWI sought a judicial review of RtR on the basis it is a discriminatory practice and inhibits the right to respect for private and family life.

At first the High Court initially found that RtR had a 'disproportionately discriminatory effect'.[53] However, following an appeal by the Home Office, judges ruled that the scheme was not inherently discriminatory and that any discriminatory behaviour exhibited by landlords was a 'proportionate means of achieving [the] legitimate aim' outlined in the Immigration Act 2014.[54] The JCWI contested the idea that RtR was forcing non-citizens to leave the country – though this was in fact the intended purpose of the policy.[55] This view was also held by David Bolt and reflected in the lack of monitoring of RtR's effectiveness by the Home Office.[56] This made all the more jarring the appeal ruling which found in favour of the Home Office on the basis that RtR had made 'some' contribution to curbing irregular migration, despite this being by the admission of the judges 'difficult to quantify'.[57]

*Right to Work*

Right to work (RtW) checks were extended and consolidated through the Immigration Act 2014 and 2016. However, restrictions on accessing employment already existed beginning with the Immigration Act (1971) where the offence of 'illegal working' was established, connecting the right to work and immigration status. The Immigration, Asylum and Nationality Act (1996) saw the introduction of the offence of employing an 'illegal worker' placing restrictions on refugees and asylum seekers applying for status, from working. These restrictions were updated in the Immigration, Asylum and Nationality Act (2006) requiring employers to undertake document checks to determine eligibility to work. Employers would now have to ensure they did not *knowingly* hire ineligible workers by undertaking checks to establish eligibility. Checks were aimed at irregular migrants, those applying for refugee and asylum status and EEA nationals from Romania and Bulgaria. This updated legislation could see employers being fined up to £2,000 (later rising from £10,000 to £20,000) for each irregular worker hired knowingly and up to two years imprisonment.[58]

The Immigration Acts' 2014 and 2016 consolidated pre-existing restrictions by shifting the burden of proof further to demonstrate the eligibility to work onto employers and employees. Under current legislation, employers may now be prosecuted if there was a 'reasonable cause' to believe that a worker was ineligible to work.[59] This means even if an employer had *unknowingly* hired an ineligible worker where proof of ineligibility did not exist, they could still be liable for up to five years imprisonment.[60] The threshold for taking criminal proceedings against employers were significantly reduced as a result of new legislation. Employees undertaking 'illegal working' could be imprisoned for up to six months and have their earnings seized from them. These changes were also accompanied by greater punitive powers bestowed on the Home Office including the right to enter business premises to undertake searches and to seize documents.

One of the most visible aspects of enforcing RtW have been immigration raids in places of work. Between 2015 and 2019, there were 44,225 immigration raids in places of work, which included South Asian and Chinese takeaways as well as care homes.[61] Immigration raids in care homes, which were in the eye of the storm during the Coronavirus pandemic, also continued through this period.[62] The Institute for Public Policy Research (IPPR) has argued that raids on restaurants and takeaways were usually precipitated by tip offs from the public, who considered certain nationalities to be removable.[63] Danny Wong, the chairperson of the Chinese Chambers for Commerce in Northern

Ireland, claimed that Chinese businesses were regarded as an 'easy target' for immigration enforcement raids.[64]

According to the Migration Observatory there is a growing demand for social care to meet the needs of Britain's ageing population, a trend which looks set to only intensify.[65] However, there has been a reduction in spending on social care since 2009, and a stark reliance on migrant labour to make up the shortfall of care workers in what is a poorly regulated, low paid and – in light of the Covid-19 pandemic – increasingly risky sector. Flows of labour for the social care sector are also being restricted through immigration laws which place limits on the ability of so-called 'low skilled' workers to come to Britain. These very same limits are also impacting on the recruitment of workers for Britain's curry houses, which are closing down in part due to a lack of staff.[66]

The contradictions in immigration policy on the one hand and the decline of publicly funded social care on the other is a good example of the intersecting crises this book is engaging with. Austerity has led to a reduction in spending on public services and in this setting the contest over who is entitled to these increasingly scant provisions is determined by who is considered British. This is even though the very care of British citizens depends on non-citizens working in deeply exploitative conditions. In many respects this is the story of British colonialism: the exploitation of racialised populations for the enrichment and service of a racially dominant group who will marginalise and exclude those on whom they depend for their very life.

Unsurprisingly then, even prior to the emergence of the hostile environment as a Conservative-led policy agenda, status checks for employment were already impacting on postcolonial citizens without passports. Employers asking for documents led to postcolonial citizens losing jobs or being unable to find them, and setting off a chain reaction of disentitlement in other areas of their life. This included being unable to claim welfare benefits or legal aid to navigate a fast-changing immigration environment as the Legal Action Group work on 'surprised Brits' showed. This trend was only set to intensify over the next few years culminating in the Windrush 'scandal' four years later in 2018.

## Accessing the NHS

The final hostile environment immigration control to be examined is the Home Office's database, the Status Verification and Enquiries Checking (SVEC) which determines eligibility to access NHS services. The denial of life-saving care to British citizens affected by immigration controls in healthcare was considered to be one of the most egregious aspects of the Windrush scandal. According to Liberty, 'All migrants in the UK are entitled to free primary healthcare and accident and emergency (A&E) treatment, as well as family planning (excluding termination of pregnancy) or treatment in secure mental health settings.'[67] However, beyond this 'most migrants are charged for most other kinds of treatment', with temporary workers and students paying the notorious NHS surcharge of up to £624.

The health surcharge proved especially controversial in the Coronavirus pandemic, when doctors, nurses and other NHS workers feted as national heroes were seen to be unfairly affected by this measure. In May 2020, the Prime Minister Boris Johnson made a pledge that NHS staff and care workers could apply for a reimbursement. This miserly gesture did not obscure the deadly impact of the pandemic, which disproportionately led to the deaths of postcolonial citizens and non-citizens working in health and social care.[68] While many were preoccupied with the supposed 'biological' reasons for the racialised impact of the pandemic, structural racism featured less prominently in such debates. In sum, these neglected structural factors were that the immigration controls determining access to healthcare also apply to NHS workers, forming part of the same continuum of racial violence which puts these workers at an increased risk of harm and premature death.

The immigration controls embedded in the NHS can also be understood through the context of moral panics around 'health tourism'. As part of the wider anti-immigration discourse in British political life, a narrative emerged in which migrants were accused of coming to Britain in order to access free healthcare. The NHS is a publicly funded good which is underpinned by the idea it is 'free at the point of delivery' but has been subject to neoliberal reforms including piecemeal privatisation and the introduction of an 'internal market'. The multiple pressures on the NHS and its parlous state have been channelled through the figure of the 'health tourist' who bears more than a passing resemblance to the 'benefit scrounger'. Health tourism was used as a reason to justify the NHS surcharge as well as increasing charges for a wider range of services.

While politicians argue that the hostile environment is targeted at 'illegal immigrants', this chapter has shown that this framing obscures some important realities. Firstly, the border violence directed at non-citizens operates on a continuum with border violence experienced by Britain's postcolonial citizens. The Windrush scandal was not an accident so much as the product of immigration legislation which has historically served to keep out, deter and increasingly complicate access to British citizenship for formerly colonised populations. Secondly, the Immigration Acts of 2014 and 2016 have embedded border controls into the institutions of everyday life whether these are schools or hospitals, the job centre or places of work.

Again, the Windrush scandal showed how people who had arrived in Britain through legal means were made into non-citizens by lack of paperwork. Britain's postcolonial citizens were more likely to be caught up in immigration checks because they – in the words of a government minister – 'looked foreign', leading to disastrous outcomes for many. Finally, debates about immigration and citizenship cannot be separated from who is considered *deserving* of national resources. Non-citizens and Britain's postcolonial citizens are framed as drains on public goods to which they have not contributed but which they are seen as coming to Britain to exploit. The next chapter will dig deeper into this history of how making a racial hierarchy of citizenship helps to keep Britain white.

# 5

# Hierarchies of Citizenship
# in White Britain

The British Empire was a vehicle for establishing, maintaining and justifying White supremacy on a global scale, and for persuading generations of Britons that ours is a White island that keeps colonised subjects of colour in their place overseas.

Alan Lester[1]

For the minority people from as long as I can remember, there's always been that hostile environment, so it's nothing new. It's not just something that happens since whoever made that statement about creating a hostile environment. It had always been a hostile environment where I'm concerned from the 1960s when I came to the UK until now. It got *more* hostile, when that statement was made . . .

72-year-old 'Bill' who moved from
Jamaica to Britain in the 1960s.[2]

The Prevent strategy and the hostile environment are both varieties of border violence operating in the service of keeping Britain white. The idea of Britain as a white nation rather than a white empire took shape through the process of post-war decolonisation. Britishness as whiteness translated into a concrete racial hierarchy of citizenship through which some citizens became considered more 'British' than others. The everyday racial bordering of Muslim citizens pioneered through Prevent prefigured the emergence of the hostile environment by offering up an example of how undesirable others in the white British home could be detected, contained and removed. All the while, the same government department has been at the centre of both terrorism and immigration policy: the Home Office. Its website declares that 'The first duty of the government is to keep citizens safe and the country secure.'[3] Keeping Britain 'safe' is the work of keeping out or removing racialised others deemed to be dangerous or undeserving of citizenship or both.

Whether it is the terrorist who comes to harm us or the migrant who comes to exploit us and whether they arrive by boat across the channel or have lived here all their lives, these are the figures against whom border violence is directed. This book has shown how the Prevent strategy introduced the everyday borders of 'Britishness' which Muslim populations must navigate to show they are not an extremist threat to Britain. For Muslims, the entitlements of citizenship have been made conditional on the successful crossing of these everyday borders from the threatening borderlands of 'Muslim ghettos' to the safety of Britishness. The same logic underpins the hostile environment: the racialisation of groups of people resident in Britain, considered to be a drain on national resources rightfully belonging to (white) Britons, who have to navigate everyday borders in order to access public goods.

This chapter examines in greater detail the historical context of how racial hierarchies of citizenship in Britain were made possible. This means locating Prevent and the hostile environment in a longer history of border violence enacted through immigration laws which have been directed at Britain's postcolonial citizens and their ancestors. This border violence is connected to the conflicts within the British Empire, which ruled over Black and brown populations by upholding a theoretical idea of equality between subjects, but which was rendered practically void by the racial differentiation which marked colonial rule. These histories inform us about the different ways in which the movement of Black and brown British subjects to the metropole and white setter colonies was restricted. They are also instructive for how the movement of white populations between white settler colonies like Australia, New Zealand and Canada and the British metropole was made comparatively easy.

This chapter draws on Luke de Noronha's idea of differential (im) mobilities and Nadine El-Enany's view of dispossession, to consider more closely the functions of Prevent and the hostile environment as examples of everyday racial bordering.[4] The ideas of (im)mobility and dispossession draw our attention to how Britain's postcolonial citizens have long been subject to border violence in an effort to keep Britain white, even where they were able to successfully obtain citizenship. Both the differential experience of acquiring citizenship and then accessing the rights and entitlements of being a British citizen speak to the realities of long-standing racial hierarchies of citizenship. These racial hierarchies are being remade in the present through counter-terrorism and immigration legislation. Finally, the chapter also draws on the Windrush Lessons Learned Review (WLLR) to assess how imperial amnesia is embodied in the burden of proof required to gain access to British citizenship.

### Race, borders and citizenship hierarchies

Speaking in 1982, Ambalavaner Sivanandan, who was a leading thinker on 'race', colonialism and capitalism, underlined unequivocally what is at stake in resisting Britain's immigration regimes. He said,

> I don't care whether a police officer is racist, or an immigration officer is racist. Those things don't matter to me. I want the policeman punished for his racism. I want the immigration officers' laws changed so he doesn't examine my sister for her virginity when she comes to this country.[5]

Once more, in this phase of particularly vicious border work there has been a groundswell of activism and scholarship on how to understand, organise against and dismantle border violence. Sivanandan argues it is not whether a few individuals in positions of power are guilty of racism that can be addressed through racial awareness training, or what he describes as 'potty training for whites'.[6] Rather, it is that the very purpose of bordering itself is to mark racial differentiations between different British citizens, and between British citizens and non-citizens.

The literature on immigration as a practice of racial differentiation tends to focus on the legislation governing post-1945 migration to

Britain.[7] Aside from the analysis of Immigration Acts 2014 and 2016 in the previous chapter, this book has largely been concerned with the colonial and racial logics which underpin Britain's post-war immigration legislation. In the epigraph above, Alan Lester notes that colonial ideas of Britain as a white island have generated a view that Britain's postcolonial citizens are not *really* British and are in fact from elsewhere. As Reiko Karatani underlines, it was not formal membership of the British Empire and later of the British Commonwealth that determined belonging, but that 'Britishness' as a national identity was secured through immigration policies.[8] Immigration law served 'to denote who "belonged" to Britain' and it was these policies that materialised the idea of Britishness as whiteness.[9] Immigration law has thereby been a means to deter, keep out and remove Britain's subjects of colour from the nation.

The territorial expansion of the British Empire included Black and brown people as colonial subjects, but the desire to keep Britain white underpinned the use of immigration legislation to meet these ends. Through the process of decolonisation we see that 'citizenship, in combination with immigration laws, constitutes the official expression of who is deemed a legitimate member of the political unit and on what terms'.[10] It is unsurprising that, as Elsa Oommen's research shows, historic immigration restrictions placed on non-white Commonwealth citizens and subjects already constituted an 'unofficial hostile environment'.[11] As the words of 'Bill' make clear in the epigraph to this chapter, the hostile environment is not the shocking self-contained moment of injustice it is portrayed to be in Amelia Gentleman's *The Windrush Betrayal*. Instead, it is the continuation and intensification of hostility towards Britain's postcolonial citizens which has always been a feature of life in Britain. The hostile environment, as Oommen exclaims, 'has always been with us!'

If British citizenship is shaped by the history of racial differentiation, then it follows that the experience of British citizenship held by postcolonial citizens is one marked by racism. As De Noronha writes,

Citizens who are negatively racialised – defined as minorities, outsiders and foreigners despite their legal membership – do not enjoy full membership or homey belonging. They tend to be discriminated against by different institutions of the state, have unequal access to employment, housing and healthcare, and to be vulnerable to racist violence in public space.[12]

With this in mind there are two core logics of immigration legislation that must be considered to clarify how Prevent and the hostile environment fit into the ongoing work of keeping Britain white. The first aspect of this is immigration as the racialized restriction of movement and the second is thinking about immigration as a form of dispossession. Prevent and the hostile environment function to immobilise and dispossess Britain's postcolonial citizens through everyday racial bordering. Through these two types of racial bordering which have emerged from different policy areas (counter-terrorism and immigration) and different political issues like terrorism and migration, we see the production of hierarchies of citizenship in which the histories of colonial racial differentiation are kept alive.

### Differential immobility

De Noronha's *Deporting Black Britons* is an account of the euphemistically labelled 'removal' or 'return' from Britain to Jamaica of four black men with criminal records. Rather than focusing on the 'deserving' victims of the Windrush scandal who had been deported, de Noronha chooses to write about people with criminal records in order to understand how it is through 'the connections between punitive criminal justice policies and aggressive immigration restrictions – that we can develop a more expansive account of state racism'.[13] What emerges is a complex and devastating account of deportation as a 'routine and unremarkable element of immigration policy'.[14] While this book focuses on British citizens and how they are susceptible to racial bordering practices including citizenship deprivation and deportation, de Noronha's focus on the deportability of non-citizens is still profoundly instructive.

Firstly, it is another important reminder that the violence of racial bordering is experienced on a continuum that ranges from non-citizens to citizens in multi-status Britain. Secondly, the idea of deportability highlights the structural conditions which have meant that the four men at the centre of *Deporting Black Britons* were placed at greater risk of deportation. Between the criminalisation of Black men through policing, the criminal justice system, and the anti-Black histories of British immigration regimes, deportability captures another set of intersecting policy areas which operate to keep Britain white. Thirdly, and most importantly for the analysis presented here, deportability is an expression of the differential ability of Black and brown people to move freely from formerly colonised spaces, to gain entry *and to stay put* in former metropoles.

De Noronha argues, 'Who gets to move is always a racial question, and differential (im)mobilities both reflect and constitute racial distinctions. If blackness has been defined by particularly enduring forms of unfreedom, then this unfreedom has been about the inability to move freely.'[15] In this sense deportation represents the acute precarity of life as Black citizens and non-citizens in Britain, insofar as you can always be 'sent back' – a form of unfreedom even if you were able to gain admittance in spite of immigration restrictions. This precarity of belonging also echoes citizenship deprivation orders directed at Muslim citizens like Shamima Begum on the basis of national security concerns. As de Noronha points out, 'deportable citizens racialised as black and brown, [...] often hail from the same countries as the UK's largest "ethnic minorities".'[16] This insight makes the Windrush scandal and citizenship deprivation experienced by Muslims appear less anomalous and more part of a continuum of border violence aimed at Britain's postcolonial citizens.

Differential (im)mobility is one of the key logics underpinning immigration regimes, particularly those which govern movement from the Global South to the Global North. Leah Cowan has shown in her work *Border Nation* how this restriction of movement is fundamentally tied up with structures of global capitalism, which encourage the flow of goods and capital but not the people who have been exploited in their production.[17] Therefore, from de Noronha's perspective global regimes of citizenship are then simply a way of enshrining these inequalities between nations by regulating population flows between them.

Differential (im)mobilities also animate the hostile environment and the Prevent strategy in Britain through the practices of detention and deportation afflicting those made into non-citizens. It may now be routine to detain and deport people, but these are still some of the most explicitly violent and financially lucrative aspects of the state's ability to enforce borders.[18] As Cowan notes, detention centres are run by hugely profitable global private security companies like GEO Group, G4S and Serco.[19]

Britain currently has 14 immigration detention centres, which form part of the Home Office Detention Estate where those who have fallen foul of the hostile environment (including pregnant people and children) are detained under the presumption of being non-citizens who will be 'returned'. The deportation of British citizens convicted of or accused of terrorism offences is generally presaged by citizenship deprivation. Many instances of citizenship deprivation have occurred when British citizens were not physically in Britain such as the case of Somali-born Mahdi Hashi who arrived in Britain as a child with his family as an asylum seeker and eventually gained citizenship. As a teenager he accused MI5 of harassing him to become an informer and was later made stateless while on a visit to Somalia.[20] Hashi was rendered by the US and detained by the CIA; eventually he was prosecuted and imprisoned in the US accused of joining the Somali group, al-Shabab. Aid workers Tauqir Sharif and Shakiel Shabir were meanwhile made stateless after they travelled to Syria to provide humanitarian assistance, blocking their return to Britain on the grounds they posed a risk to 'national security'.[21]

The further refusal to repatriate British women and children from Syrian refugee camps and to instead deprive them of their citizenship has been described as the state's abandonment of people to death and torture.[22] Over the last 15 years the British state has made it progressively easier for the Home Secretary to enact citizenship deprivation through the use of secret evidence, limiting rights of appeal and normalising the risk of statelessness. The Nationality and Borders Act means the state no longer has to notify people who are subject to citizenship deprivation. The inability to move around freely outside of Britain was also a key outcome of the hostile environment for postcolonial citizens. An example of this loss of freedom was exemplified when postcolonial citizens visiting Jamaica, Trinidad, India, Pakistan and Bangladesh were stopped from re-entering Britain because they did not have a British passport or an Indefinite Leave to Remain (ILR) stamp on an existing passport.

There are other practices which fall short of detention and deportation that neverthless constitute everyday differential (im)mobility for Britain's postcolonial citizens through counter-terrorism and immigration. Examples include pre-emptive counter-terrorism measures such as control orders which were later replaced by Terrorism Prevention and Investigation Measures (TPIMs). Cerie Bullivant was placed under a control order on the basis of secret evidence which he has never seen and that required him to wear a security tag and regularly report to the police. Bullivant's life under a control order meant he was forced to drop out of college and was unable to find a job. His attempts to undertake a nursery degree were similarly upended, 'They wouldn't change my signing-on times. You do six weeks of university study and then six weeks out as a student nurse in hospitals – trying to do shift work without them changing my signing-in times meant it was never going to happen.'[23] TPIMs went further than control orders because as a form of 'internal exile' they could force subjects to relocate to another part of Britain with 'restrictions on the distance they can be moved and the size of the area within which they are allowed to travel.'[24]

The hostile environment has engendered similar effects for postcolonial citizens. Terms such as being 'stranded', being in 'limbo' and being 'stuck' have been used to capture the sense of paralysis that overtakes life once a failed immigration check has set in motion a chain reaction of disentitlement. The loss of a job, the inability to access healthcare, the cessation of welfare benefits, the loss of a rented home, and the loss of access to banking services are just a few of the ways the hostile environment serves to limit mobility. The demand to check in at set times at

Immigration Reporting Centres located far from where you live echoes the use of control orders. Waiting to be arrested and waiting to be deported are themselves a traumatic prospect resulting in immobility. As the late Windrush campaigner Paulette Wilson said about the threat of deportation looming over her, 'I couldn't eat or sleep'.[25] (Im)mobility can thus be understood as an embodied experience felt by those toward whom racial border violence is directed, which words such as 'stranded', 'limbo' and 'stuck' attempt to name.

The loss of the freedom to move about in everyday life is experienced in everything from the loss of freedom to live in your home, to go to work, to visit a GP or hospital, to the loss of driving a car and everything else besides. In *Chasing Status*, 'Alicia' says 'All my friends started driving, going to uni. This made me realise that without this piece of paper, I'm no one. I went into a depression then'.[26] Later she notes, 'your teachers and your friends are telling you "we're going to go on holiday; we're going to travel; we're going to go away". And it just daunts you, like, I'll never be able to do anything like that'.[27] The lack of agency and the sense of being subject to the support and kindness of friends and family to survive in the face of (im)mobility, further underscores a loss of freedom to move about on your own terms. The limited means through which to challenge the loss of freedom to move further compound the sense of being stuck in a form of internal exile.

It is unsurprising that in her review of the Windrush scandal Wendy Williams argues that people have been 'trapped by the hostile environment policy net'.[28] The word 'trap' is a byword for 'immobility' because it captures the cruel efficacy of the Immigration Acts of 2014 and 2016 in creating a state of everyday paralysis where your ability to live life is stripped away piece by piece. The case of Jocelyn John illustrates the effect of (im)mobility which is the 'voluntary' self-removal of those who can no longer move about in order to live.[29] John travelled from Grenada to Britain at the age of four on her mother's passport and later lost her own Grenadian passport with the ILR stamp. Unable to apply for a new passport despite the wealth of evidence attesting to her life in Britain, John lost her job and was made homeless, relying on friends and staying at hostels. Incited by the fear of forced deportation and in light of Operation Vaken's 'Go Home' vans, John left Britain in 2016 to travel to Grenada on a flight booked by the Home Office. Differential (im)mobility has been extended into everyday life through the hostile environment in order to facilitate the removal, either forced or 'voluntary' of Black and brown people from Britain.

### Dispossession through disentitlement

Racial bordering not only serves to immobilise Britain's postcolonial citizens and non-citizens, but it also seeks to dispossess them. This is the contention of Nadine El-Enany's *Bordering Britain* in which the author shows how immigration regimes don't simply curtail the free movement of Black and brown people from the Global South to the Global North but also serve as a form of modern day appropriation.[30] Immigration legislation central to defining the transformation of Britain's identity from an empire to a white nation limited the ability of formerly colonised populations from accessing wealth that had been accumulated at their expense. Instead this wealth came to be seen as the rightful property of white Britons and was enforced through immigration legislation which defined Britishness as whiteness. El-Enany writes,

> the 1981 British Nationality Act, which raised for the first time the spectre of a post-imperial, territorially defined and circumscribed Britain. It severed a notionally white, geographically distinct Britain from its colonies and Commonwealth [...] A territorially distinct Britain and a concept of citizenship that made **Britishness commensurate with whiteness** made it clear that Britain, the landmass and everything within it, belongs to Britons, conceived intrinsically as white.[31]

This 'colonial manoeuvre' represents a 'final seizure of wealth and infrastructure secured through centuries of colonial conquest'.[32] On this basis Britain's immigration regimes must 'be understood as being on a continuum of colonialism. It is through immigration law's policing of access to colonial spoils that the racial project of capitalist accumulation is maintained'.[33] For El-Enany colonialism is not something that happened long ago in the past and somewhere else (somewhere that is not white), but is alive and kicking in the formation of Britain as a nation. Immigration legislation is once again revealed to be an important tool in fashioning a national British rooted in whiteness.

El-Enany describes Britain as a 'contemporary colonial space' closer to settler-colonial contexts than is commonly understood. Settler colonial contexts are defined by the fact that colonial appropriation is ongoing there – embodied in the marginalisation of indigenous groups – and was never formally ended. This colonial violence, which included land theft and genocide is constitutive of modern nations like the United States, Canada, Australia and New Zealand. Non-settler contexts, which typically include former metropoles of major empires including Britain, experienced a formal 'end' to empire through decolonisation and were never settled. However, for El-Enany, Britain can still be described as a colonial space precisely because the practices of dispossessing formerly colonised populations are still maintained, particularly through immigration law. Formerly colonised populations and their ancestors are kept from accessing wealth and infrastructure located in Britain that was accumulated through colonial plunder. Furthermore, the 'theft of intangibles such as economic growth and prospects, opportunities, life chances, psyches and futures' all shape the lives of formerly colonised populations.[34]

While these are key insights, there is an important caveat to this overall argument. Firstly, the politics of disentitlement – of deciding who is deserving of public goods – prefigures the dispossession of Black and brown people who already have citizenship. Earlier chapters in this book set out how the rights and entitlements of Muslim citizens and postcolonial citizens were being chipped away through Prevent and the hostile environment. From having to provide paperwork that may not exist in order to access public goods, to upholding ideas of Britishness in order to appear moderate rather than extreme, there are many ways in which non-white Britons have experienced life at the bottom of a hierarchy of citizenship. Secondly, the politics of disentitlement needs to be contextualised against a contemporary backdrop of austerity politics. At a time when public goods are being intentionally reduced through austerity policies, 'who is deserving of benefits/healthcare/education' has become an increasingly prominent question in British politics.

Prevent and the hostile environment must therefore be contextualised as part of this attempt to prevent the racialised poor from accessing national resources in times of scarcity and survival. From this perspective, the work of keeping Britain white is also being put to the service of immiserating poorer Britons and hollowing out the entitlements of citizenship for all Britons. To this extent then, dispossession as disentitlement not only impacts Britain's postcolonial citizens and non-citizens but further entrenches the power and pre-eminence of Britain's aristocratic ruling classes and their technocratic handmaidens syphoning off national resources. The decolonisation of the British Empire and its formal transition from empire to postcolonial nation gave birth to the idea of white victimhood that drives the dispossession as disentitlement. This was not the swaggering white supremacy of the British Empire but the death rattle of a former great power in terminal decline. Postcolonial Britain was riven by profound and anxious attachments to whiteness and the protection of white entitlement in a world where Britain no longer rules the waves. The idea of a white British people betrayed by elite liberal politicians allowing immigration from former colonies has held a powerful place in the post-war British imagination. What were these people doing here and why were they taking what were seen to be the rightful resources of white Britons?

### Burdens of proof on a forgetful island

Wendy Williams writes that the Windrush scandal was both 'foreseeable and avoidable'.[35] She describes how the Windrush generation was forgotten 'by those in power' and that 'a culture of disbelief and carelessness' characterised the processing of applications.[36] The remit of the report set by the home secretary was itself narrowly conceived, focusing exclusively on the experience of the Windrush generation rather than Commonwealth citizens at large, but that does not make the insights

Williams has produced any less relevant in grappling with the issue of imperial amnesia. Imperial amnesia or forgetting how postcolonial citizens arrived in Britain is connected with the cultivated disbelief about their right to be in Britain. The escalating and 'unreasonable' burden of proof required by the Home Office to process applications is underpinned by this pervasive understanding that postcolonial citizens aren't really British.[37] Conversely, the use of secret evidence and declining protections against citizenship deprivation on the grounds of national security speaks to the low threshold of evidence needed to remove postcolonial citizens from Britain.

Forgetting and disbelief work in the service of keeping Britain white, and we can see this in relation to Prevent and the hostile environment, both understood as types of racial bordering informed by the logics of (im)mobility and dispossession. Forgetting is an important political strategy in denying the claims of postcolonial citizens to their entitlements and disbelief is the conscious and ongoing attempt at making this denial concrete. As Williams writes,

> I found that some individual decision makers operated an irrational and unreasonable approach to individuals, requiring multiple documents for 'proof' of presence in the UK for each year of residence in the UK. The department has accepted that there was no basis for doing this in its own guidance.[38]

It emerges clearly in the WLLR that requirements around burden of proof were used as a political strategy to refuse citizenship applications.

This strategy is inverted in relation to the citizenship deprivation of Muslim citizens, where the Prevent strategy already presumes the idea that Muslims are a threat to Britishness. This is something that is already 'known' and therefore the diminishing standards of secret proof required to enact deprivation against Muslim citizens' and the limited means through which to appeal this, are read as common sense. For example, when the aid worker Tauqir Sharif was deprived of his citizenship, his white British wife, who also travelled to Syria, was welcome to return. He described his treatment as 'guilt by association' arguing, 'Are we really British? For me, I was always told that I was British and that whatever I do, I have equal rights to vote, to work, equal principles ... If a white colleague were to do the same as us, they wouldn't get their citizenship revoked. I find that racist'.[39] Sharif's words appear even more prescient in light of the war in Ukraine where former foreign secretary Liz Truss said she would 'absolutely' back British people seeking to fight against Russian invaders.

The burden of proof is something of a way of life, it is the task of proving your belonging in a country which has already decided you don't belong. For instance, the scramble by those affected by the hostile environment to suddenly produce evidence of their life in Britain was as devastating as it was arduous. As early as 2007, cases affecting post-colonial citizens were being flagged up for the attention of the Home Office.[40] *Chasing Status* detailed how burdens of proof were setting off chain reactions of disentitlement leading to outcomes such as the loss of jobs and homelessness.[41] In addition to this, the shock of those who felt themselves to be 'British' and therefore safe from immigration policing is a recurrent theme. People expressed disbelief that their belonging was being called into question and this sense was compounded by burdens of proof.[42]

One case flagged up in the WLLR is instructive, that of a former serviceman who 'was told he didn't have enough documentary proof of his status. He was so frightened of not being allowed back into the country that, for years, he'd refused his wife's requests for a holiday, telling her instead that he was afraid of flying'.[43] This case recalls the haunting work of Hazel Carby and the account she gives of her father's experience in an immigration interview.[44] Carl Carby came from Jamaica to Britain in 1943 as a serviceman for the RAF, choosing to remain after his marriage to a white woman named Iris. Later in 1978, Carby applied for a British passport in order that he could travel to visit family in the United States. Hazel Carby shares the following details about what happened in that interview in the Immigration and Nationality Directorate in Croydon:

My father, then fifty-seven, was interviewed by a young woman who not only insulted and intimidated him but also **accused him of lying**, of being 'an illegal immigrant', one of those who had 'sneaked into the country, landing at night on the Essex coast with a boatload of other illegals'. This representative of British immigration declared that all his records, including his RAF record and original passport, were **probably forgeries**. This was an absurd accusation. I knew that in the face of this racist rant my father would have maintained his dignity, making no demands to see a superior official, not complaining and raising his voice. He just bent to pick up his papers, which the interviewer had swept off the desk in a **wild gesture of incredulity**. Once gathered, he did not look at her again but stood with his head held high, turned his back to her, walked out of the office and left the building.[45]

Firstly, despite the fact both Carl Carby and the gentleman cited in the WLLR had been servicemen in the British Armed Forces, this was not enough either to allay either man's fears about having to 'prove' their belonging or the sneering disbelief of a British immigration officer. Secondly, the fact that in 1978 Carby was accused of lying and producing forgeries by an immigration officer who quite literally swept away the proofs of entitlement to a British passport, underlines how disbelief in enforcing immigration is a long-standing and consciously cultivated component of racial exclusion. Imperial amnesia is not an unfortunate, accidental forgetting in the manner implied by the WLLR, where the effects of racially discriminatory (historic) immigration legislation could be 'corrected' in the present if only this history was adequately remembered.[46] The refusal to remember is a political strategy as the recent scandals engulfing the home office have shown.

The 'institutionally forgotten' Windrush generation were not simply 'caught up in measures designed for people who have no right to be in the UK'.[47] They were subjects of the crown who the British state desperately sought to keep out and whose descendants are being kept out through the severing of the past from the present. The disbelief encountered by Carl Carby decades ago is of the same order as that which is experienced by the postcolonial citizens and non-citizens in the present day. It was and remains grounded in the very simple view that Britishness is synonymous with whiteness and those who contradict this fiction are, in the words of Hazel Carby, an 'oxymoron' forever haunted by the question 'Where are you from'?[48] Indeed, when the Home Office destroyed thousands of landing cards of those who travelled from the Caribbean to Britain in the 1950s and 60s, providing proof of entitlement to ILR, it highlighted the precariousness of the relationship between Britain and its postcolonial citizens.

This precariousness is tied to the lack of state record-keeping and the active destruction of records which detail the histories, journeys and stories of postcolonial citizens and their ancestors. The carelessness with which the landing cards were destroyed despite being used 'routinely' in decision-making processes regarding immigration status embodies the lack of care extended to postcolonial citizens. Furthermore, those who were worst affected by the hostile environment were often without passports for one reason or another. They had travelled to Britain on the passport of a relative as a child, or they had lost a passport that had an ILR stamp, or they had never applied for a British passport. The significance of the lack of a passport is not to be regarded as a problem in itself but as emblematic of the terse relationship between Britain and its Black and brown citizens, buttressed by disbelief and liable to rupture or break at any time. Hazel Carby's work of reconstructing her family history between the two islands of Jamaica and Britain is organised in terms of 'inventories' and 'accounting' in an effort to preserve and share which would otherwise have remained hidden.

Finally, the virginity tests to which Sivanandan was referring also exemplify the logics of disbelief and immigration. In 1979, it was discovered that virginity tests were being performed by doctors on South Asian women arriving at Heathrow Airport as fiancées to British citizens. Fiancées did not need a visa to enter Britain if they married within three months of their arrival, unlike married women who would require a visa. If women were found to be 'virgo intacta' this was taken as proof of the fact that they weren't already married. If it was determined that they were not virgins, then they were refused entry. This example is echoed in more contemporary demands from British border agents for LGBTQIA+ asylum seekers to 'prove' their sexuality by being compelled to provide 'photographic and video evidence of highly personal sexual activity'.[49]

The development of racial hierarchies of citizenship is a long-standing issue in postcolonial Britain where the process of decolonisation saw the British state effectively pulling up the drawbridge. From making it increasingly difficult for formerly colonised populations from travelling to and settling in Britain, to making the lives of postcolonial citizens difficult through differential access to public goods such as employment, healthcare and education, the racial hierarchies of citizenship have had many faces. The Prevent Strategy and the hostile environment are simply contemporary iterations of everyday racial bordering which marks out Britain's postcolonial citizens as not *really* British. Both these policy areas which speak to distinctive political issues like terrorism and migration mark out Black and brown citizens as suspect in different ways.

As forms of everyday racial bordering, Prevent and the hostile environment work in tandem to weaken the ability of postcolonial citizens to remain in Britain and to access their rights and entitlements. When a 17-year-old Black British boy who is non-verbal went missing from a hospital in 2022, he was arrested by British Transport Police and ended up in a deportation centre marked for 'removal'.[50] He was described as being Nigerian and had been unable to provide proof of his right to be in Britain. When his mother eventually located him, it transpired he had never left the country and those officials had simply assumed that he was a Nigerian national and in Britain illegally. This story embodies the horrifying end logic of everyday racial borders: as a postcolonial citizen you can never feel safe in your belonging.

# Concluding thoughts: The diminishing wages of whiteness

Let's face it, whiteness isn't worth what it used to be worth. Its value is falling globally.

Paul Gilroy[1]

Reactionary nationalism is mobilised for political gain, and migrants, whether constructed as workers or scroungers, documented or illegal, have shouldered much of the blame for finance capitalism's fiscal calamities. A nostalgia for empire and the euphoria of world war victory has displaced demands for a return to post-war welfarism.

Gargi Bhattacharyya et al.[2]

This book has charted the ways in which counter-terrorism and immigration policies operate as mutually reinforcing agendas which remake, police and enforce the borders of white Britain. This violence of Britishness has ostensibly operated as the postcolonial defence of national borders and resources seen as the rightful inheritance of white Britons from those racialised as perpetual outsiders. In parcelling out who among the citizenry is 'deserving' of the rights and entitlements of citizenship, the multiple and expanding routes to disentitlement are laid bare. But this violence of Britishness doesn't just harm postcolonial citizens and non-citizens. As Paul Gilroy notes, whiteness no longer provides the kind of returns to those who are its intended beneficiaries but rather, as this book has argued, contributes to their immiseration through the broadening of disentitlement. As the authors of *Empire's Endgame* point out, 'Britain is not a happy place'. Never had this been truer than in this current cost-of-living crisis where skyrocketing energy bills, high inflation and stagnating wages underline a sense of accelerating decline.[3]

Historically, Britishness as whiteness has relied on the post-war racial and class compact of shared national resources where – at least theoretically – everyone in the national home was taken care of through the welfare state and public goods like the NHS.[4] Think of *Downton Abbey*, home to a benign British aristocrat; somewhere where the white characters know their place (whether it is upstairs or downstairs) and its residents are looked after through vast amounts of mysteriously acquired if unevenly distributed wealth. Similarly, a post-war national compact provided a modest redistribution of colonial wealth which benefited working class populations in Britain who had hitherto been excluded, brutalised and downtrodden. Their radical history of revolutionary zeal, riots and reform is now a mere footnote in the national story revealing the extent of Britain's amnesia about its past.[5] Nonetheless, this national compact was not intended for postcolonial citizens on whose backs and whose ancestor's backs, colonial wealth was accrued. Valluvan writes that 'Western capitalism' is 'reneging on some of the key promises of the *trente glorieuses* (1946-75)' or that the national compact is no longer working.[6]

While El-Enany argues that Britain 'is the place where colonial spoils are located', in fact its public infrastructure, which embodied the redistribution of those spoils, is being systematically dismantled. This is thanks to the neoliberal 'rollback' of the welfare state, a process which was ignited by Margaret Thatcher in the 1980s and has been sustained by her ideological heirs from Tony Blair to Liz Truss. While neoliberal reforms were initially tested in African and South American states in need of IMF loans attached to structural adjustment programmes, or through Western support for militarised authoritarian governments, its ravages are now being seen in metropoles that historically were protected through their ill-gotten colonial gains.

Kojo Koram, drawing on the work of Aimé Césaire, talks about these changes in terms of a 'boomerang effect' according to which 'experiments carried out in the peripheries of the empire eventually come flying back to its very heartland'.[7] This 'cost-of-living crisis' as it is being described in Britain today is simply what life has been like in the non-Western hinterlands of capitalism, colonialism and racism, and it is here to stay in the absence of radical change.

Koram also brings into view how 'In the era of globalisation, Britain has consistently stood out as the most unequal of the "advanced" European countries' where income and wealth inequality is pervasive.[8] A long regime of austerity, the effects of Brexit and the Covid-19 epidemic have all taken their toll on Britain. As Gargi Bhattacharyya et al. outline,

> the NHS and council homes that defined the boom years of the 1950s and 1960s are being privatised and stripped to the bone, accelerating the crises in housing, health, and social care. The austerity imposed on other parts of the welfare state which followed the 2008 financial crisis has brought increasing hardship and frustration, through both a lack of services and cuts to public sector jobs. On top of this, a deregulated labour market, zero-hour contracts and the gig economy mean that work, if you can get it, is precarious and low paid.[9]

If Brexit was about 'taking back control' of borders, then this also included the right to decide how to distribute alarmingly diminished national resources. For Danny Dorling, this logic is best exemplified by the fictitious but powerful claims by the Vote Leave campaign regarding the £350 million pounds per week for the NHS which would be gained by leaving the EU. He argued this promise appealed to elderly white middle class voters suffering from a 'decline in health' and 'mortality rise' due to austerity which 'had played a major role in the rapid worsening of overall UK public health'.[10] Therefore, the wages of whiteness – the economic, social and psychological ways in which white Britons benefit from *and aspire to benefit from* their status, is not the lucrative business that it once was. The public goods regarded as the preserve of white Britons have been plundered by the descendants of colonial ruling classes exemplified by the Bullingdon Club and the 'opportunistic coterie of managers, consultants and plutocrats' who have been abetted by the rise of neoliberal politics.[11] As Gilroy puts it, the 'Conservatives' bleak assertion that there is no alternative way of living, governing and organising social life' has seemingly triumphed.[12]

In this context of inequality and the plunder of public wealth by a wealthy elite, everyday racial bordering which determines differential access to the entitlements of citizenship is being sold as a form of political salvation for the nation. Britishness as a postcolonial violence entails a promise to rescue deserving white British populations from the machinations of undeserving populations. Only then can there be a return to the halcyon days of an unspoilt white Britain in which everyone knew their place, whether this was upstairs or downstairs. Everyday racial bordering as a form of disentitlement which has impacted Britons postcolonial citizens is serving as the basis for a renewed white compact. From Brexit to an unprecedented majority of 80 seats in the 2019 General Election for Boris Johnson's Conservatives who promised to 'get Brexit done', the politics of taking back control from the racialised menace threatening British borders and resources has proved a powerful electoral strategy promising the reinstatement of the primacy of white Britons.

However, the gap between what has been tacitly promised to white Britons and the reality of life in Britain, where choosing between whether you eat or heat your home is increasingly commonplace, taking back control is turning out to be something of a pyrrhic victory. The wages of whiteness overwhelmingly benefit a small plutocratic class rather than white Britons at large. The disentitlement experienced predominantly by Britain's Black and brown citizens' spells trouble for us all. The violence of Britishness does not promise salvation through better public services, education or jobs and these are not even issues that any of the main political parties – including the Labour Party – appear to be campaigning on. In fact, if taking back control has meant anything, it is the strengthening of authoritarianism and the police power reflected in the Police, Crime, Sentencing and Courts Act (2022) which diminishes the right to protest as well as expanding police powers in the policing of Gypsy, Roma and Traveller populations. We have a hollowed-out politics of the echo chamber in which racist policies backed by carceral state power and glib slogans are replacing the actual work of governing Britain.

When the ECHR successfully grounded the first flight meant to deport asylum seekers from Britain to Rwanda, the *Guardian* columnist Marina Hyde suggested this latest attempt at 'culture wars' was intended to 'annoy the right people' and echoed a 'source close to government thinking' that it was never meant to take off.[13] Attempts to dismiss border violence and its devastating effects on those targeted for deportation as 'culture wars' designed to distract from the real issues fatally misunderstand both the logic of these policies and what they signify in British politics today. Border violence is not cheap: it is backed by expensive, punitive and wide-ranging measures. Border violence offers a spectacular return on whiteness, a big show that the government is doing 'something' to help its more deserving citizens even if it won't help them feed their children or warm their homes. Border violence is not a trick behind which the real work of devastating what's left of Britain's public infrastructure, laws and democracy happens; it has become one of the primary vehicles through which such violence is perpetrated.

# Notes

## Introduction

1.  Paul Gilroy, *Ain't no Black in the Union Jack* (London: Verso Books, 2002), p.xxxvii.
2.  Richard Kerbaj, *The Secret History of the Five Eyes: The Untold Story of the Shadowy International Spy Network, Through Its Targets, Traitors and Spies* (London: Bonnier Books, 2022).
3.  'Factbox: Europeans who joined Islamic State', *Reuters*, 29 February 2019, www.reuters.com/article/us-mideast-crisis-islamic-state-prisoner-idUSKCN1Q81EO (last accessed December 2022).
4.  Owen Bowcatt, 'Shamima Begum Loses First Stage of Appeal Against Citizenship Removal', *Guardian* (7 February 2020), www.theguardian.com/uk-news/2020/feb/07/shamima-begum-loses-appeal-against-removal-of-citizenship, (accessed May 2022).
5.  Amelia Gentleman, '"My Life is in Ruins": Wrongly Deported Windrush People Facing Fresh Indignity', *Guardian* (10 September 2018), www.theguardian.com/uk-news/2018/sep/10/windrush-people-wrongly-deported-jamaica-criminal-offence, (accessed May 2022).
6.  Francis Webber, *The Embedding of State Hostility: A Background Paper on the Windrush Scandal* (London: Institute of Race Relations, 2018), irr.org.uk/app/uploads/2018/11/Embedding-State-hostility-v4.pdf, (accessed May 2022).
7.  'Postcolonial citizenship' is an adaptation of the idea of postcolonial people which can be found in Nasreen Ali, Barnor Hesse, and Salman Sayyid, *A Postcolonial People South Asians in Britain*, (London: Hurst Publishers, 2006).
8.  Basit Ali, 'The Government's Borders Bill Rubber-Stamps Racism', *Tribune Magazine* (December 2021), tribunemag.co.uk/2021/12/nationality-and-borders-bill-racism-clause-nine-priti-patel, (accessed June 2022).
9.  Francis Webber, *Citizenship: From Right to Privilege*, (London: Institute of Race Relations, 2022), irr.org.uk/wp-content/uploads/2022/09/Deprivation-of-citizenship-Final-LR.pdf, (last accessed September 2022).
10. Amelia Gentleman, 'Windrush Scandal Caused by "30 Years of Racist Immigration Laws" – Report', *Guardian* (29 May, 2022), www.theguardian.

com/uk-news/2022/may/29/windrush-scandal-caused-by-30-years-of-racist-immigration-laws-report, (accessed June 2022).

11. Amelia Gentleman, 'Home Office Tried to "Sanitise" Staff Education Module on Colonialism', *Guardian* (10 June 2022), www.theguardian.com/politics/2022/jun/10/home-office-tried-to-sanitise-staff-education-module-on-colonialism, (accessed June 2022).

12. Ibid.

13. Leo McKinstry, 'Shamima Begum Deserves No Sympathy from Us, Despite Her Quest for Victimhood', *Telegraph* (18 February 2018), www.telegraph.co.uk/news/2019/02/18/shamima-begum-deserves-no-sympathy-us-despite-quest-victimhood/, (accessed May 2022).

14. Roy Greenslade, 'Sajid Javid is Pandering to Right-wing Press over Shamima Begum', *Guardian* (24 February 2019), www.theguardian.com/commentisfree/2019/feb/24/sajid-javid-pander-rightwing-press-shamima-begum, (accessed May 2022).

15. twitter.com/bbcnews/status/1096178559264219138.

16. Allison Pearson, 'Let's Stop Making Excuses for these "Jihadi Brides"', *Telegraph* (25 February 2015), www.telegraph.co.uk/news/worldnews/islamic-state/11434343/Lets-stop-making-excuses-for-these-jihadi-brides.html, (accessed May 2022).

17. Grace Dent, 'If Teenage Girls Want to Join Isis in the Face of All its Atrocities, Then They Should Leave and Never Return', *Independent* (23 February 2015), www.independent.co.uk/voices/comment/if-teenage-girls-want-to-join-isis-in-the-face-of-all-its-atrocities-then-they-should-leave-and-never-return-10065516.html, (accessed May 2022).

18. Ian Drury, Jason Groove, and Inderdeep Bains, 'Fiasco that Shames Britain: Amber Rudd Faces Call to Quit as She's Forced to Admit Caribbean Migrants to Britain Could Have Been Kicked out by Mistake', *Daily Mail* (16 April 2018), www.dailymail.co.uk/news/article-5622997/Amber-Rudd-faces-call-quit.html, (accessed May 2022).

19. Michael Mann, 'The Shame, Indignation and Sadness Caused by the Windrush Scandal', *Independent* (22 April 2018), www.independent.co.uk/voices/letters/letters-windrush-antibiotics-acid-attack-a8316051.html, (accessed May 2022).

20. Pippa Crerar, 'Sajid Javid Pledges to Urgently "Do Right" by Windrush Generation', *Guardian* (30 April 2018), www.theguardian.com/uk-news/2018/apr/30/sajid-javid-pledges-to-do-right-by-windrush-generation, (accessed May 2022).

21. Kennetta Hammond-Perry, *London is the Place for Me: Black Britons, Citizenship and the Politics of Race* (Oxford: Oxford University Press, 2016).

22. BBC, 'Amber Rudd: I Was Right to Resign over Windrush Controversy', *BBC* (3 September 2018), www.bbc.co.uk/news/uk-politics-45399684, (accessed May 2022).

23. Robbie Shilliam, *Race and the Undeserving Poor: From Abolition to Brexit* (Newcastle Upon Tyne: Agenda Publishing/Columbia University Press, 2018).

24. Ibid.

25. Jamie Grierson, 'Windrush Compensation Scheme Has "Concerning Weaknesses", Says Charity', *Guardian* (15 November 2021), www. theguardian.com/uk-news/2021/nov/15/windrush-compensation-scheme-has-concerning-weaknesses-says-charity, (accessed May 2022).

26. Amelia Gentleman, 'Black Official Quit "Racist" Windrush Compensation Scheme', *Guardian* (18 November, 2020), www.theguardian.com/ uk-news/2020/nov/18/black-official-quit-allegedly-racist-windrush-compensation-scheme, (accessed May 2022).

27. Ibid.

28. Satnam Virdee, and Brendan McGeever, 'Racism, Crisis, Brexit', *Ethnic and Racial Studies*, 41(10) (2017): 1802–19, DOI: 10.1080/01419870. 2017.1361544.

29. Alana Lentin, 'Europe and the Silence about Race', *European Journal of Social Theory*, 11(4) (2008): 487–503, here p. 491. doi:10.1177/136843 1008097008.

30. Hamid Dabashi, *Europe and its Shadows; Coloniality after Empire*, (London: Pluto Press, 2019).

31. David Theo Goldberg, 'Racial Europeanization', *Ethnic and Racial Studies*, 29(2) (2006): 331–64, DOI: 10.1080/01419870500465611.

32. Ibid, p. 336.

33. Aimé Césaire, *Discourse on Colonialism* (Monthly Review Press: New York, 2000), p. 36.

34. Elizabeth Hull, *Absolute Destruction: Military Culture and the Practices of War in Imperial Germany* (Ithaca and London: Cornell University Press, 2006).

35. Elizabeth Baer, *The Genocidal Gaze; From German Southwest Africa to the Third Reich* (Detroit: Wayne State University Press, 2017).

36. David Theo Goldberg, 'Racial Europeanization', p. 336.

37. Gurminder, K. Bhambra, 'The Current Crisis of Europe: Refugees, Colonialism, and the Limits of Cosmopolitanism', *European Law Journal*, 22(05) (2017): 395–405, DOI: doi.org/10.1111/eulj.12234.

38. Alan Lester, Kate Boehme, and Peter Mitchell, *Ruling the World; Freedom, Civilisation and Liberalism in the Nineteenth Century British Empire* (Cambridge: Cambridge University Press, 2021).

39. Ibid, p. 7.
40. Ibid, pp. 8–9.
41. Bill Schwarz, *Memories of Empire, Volume I. White Man's World* (Oxford: Oxford University Press, 2011), pp. 13–18.
42. Ethics and Empire: www.mcdonaldcentre.org.uk/ethics-and-empire (accessed June 2022).
43. Georgie Wemyss, *The Invisible Empire: White Discourse, Tolerance and Belonging* (Farnham: Ashgate, 2009), p. 3.
44. Ibid, p. 12.
45. Barnor Hesse and Salman Sayyid, *Un/settled Multiculturalisms: Diasporas, Entanglements, Transruptions* (London: Zed Books, 2000), p. 218.
46. Ibid.
47. Paul Gilroy, *There Ain't no Black in the Union Jack* (Abingdon: Routledge, 2002).
48. Bill Schwarz, *Memories of Empire, Volume I.*
49. Ibid, p. 65.
50. Ibid, p. 120.
51. Ibid, p. 109.
52. Ibid, p. 10.
53. Ibid, p. 116.
54. Camilla Schofield, *Enoch Powell and the Making of Postcolonial Britain* (Cambridge: Cambridge University Press, 2013).
55. Ibid.
56. Andy Richards, 'Enoch Powell: What Was the "Rivers of Blood" Speech? Full Text Here', *Birmingham Mail* (30 March 2015), www.birminghammail.co.uk/news/midlands-news/enoch-powell-what-rivers-blood-8945556 (accessed January 2023).
57. Ibid.
58. Camilla Schofield, *Enoch Powell and the Making of Postcolonial Britain*, p. 57.
59. Ibid, p. 113.
60. Ibid, p. 78.
61. Paul Gilroy, *After Empire* (Abingdon: Routledge, 2004), p. 98.
62. Paul Gilroy, *Postcolonial Melancholia*, (New York: Columbia University Press, 2004).
63. British Pathé, *Our Jamaican Problem*, (1955), www.britishpathe.com/video/our-jamaican-problem/query/our+jamaica+problem, (accessed June 2022).
64. British Pathé, *Racial Troubles in Notting Hill*, (1959), www.britishpathe.com/video/racial-troubles-in-notting-hill/query/racial+troubles+in+notting+hill, (accessed June 2022).

65. For a critique of how fears of white replacement inform scholarship, see John Holmwood, 'Claiming Whiteness', *Ethnicities*, 20(1) (2019): 234–39.

66. Ghassan Hage, *White Nation: Fantasies of White Supremacy in a Multicultural Society* (Melbourne: Routledge in association with Pluto Press Australia, 2000), p. 166.

67. Ghassan Hage, 'The Spatial Imaginary of National Practices: Dwelling—Domesticating /Being—Exterminating', *Environment and Planning D: Society and Space*, 14(4) (1996): 463–85, here p. 479.

68. Maya Goodfellow, *Hostile Environment* (London: Verso, 2019).

69. Jamie Grierson, 'Hostile environment: Anatomy of a Policy Disaster', *Guardian* (27 August 2018), www.theguardian.com/uk-news/2018/aug/27/hostile-environment-anatomy-of-a-policy-disaster, (accessed June 2022).

70. Emblematic examples of this literature include Kenichi Ohmae, *Borderless World: Power and Strategy in the Interlinked Economy* (New York: Harper Business, 1990), and Thomas L. Friedman, *The World is Flat: A Brief History of the Twenty-First Century* (New York: Farrar, Straus and Giroux, 2005).

71. Etienne Balibar, 'Europe as Borderland', *Environment and Planning D: Society and Space*, 27(2) (2009): 190–215, doi:10.1068/d13008.

72. Nira Yuval-Davis, Georgie Wemyss and Kathryn Cassidy, *Bordering* (Cambridge: Polity Press, 2019).

73. Ibid.

74. Ibid.

75. Gargi Bhattacharyya, *Rethinking Racial Capitalism: Questions of Reproduction and Survival*, (London: Rowman and Littlefield, 2018).

76. Transparency International Uk, "Concern Over Corruption Red Flags in 20% of UK's PPE Procurement', press release (22 April 2021), www.transparency.org.uk/track-and-trace-uk-PPE-procurement-corruption-risk-VIP-lane, (accessed June 2022).

77. John-Paul Ford Rojas, 'Cost of Living Crisis: Minister Says People Could "Take on More Hours" at Work or Move to a "Better Paid Job" to Protect Themselves From Cost of Living Surge', *Sky News* (16 May 2022), news.sky.com/story/minister-says-people-should-work-more-hours-or-move-to-a-better-job-to-protect-themselves-from-cost-of-living-surge-12614360, (accessed June 2022).

78. David Roediger, *The Wages of Whiteness; Race and the Making of the American Working Class* (London: Verso, 1991).

79. W.E.B. Du Bois, *Black Reconstruction in America* (Oxford: Oxford University Press, [1935] 2014).

80. Cheryl Harris, 'Whiteness as Property', *Harvard Law Review*, 106(8) (1993): 1707–91.

81. John Narayan, 'The Wages of Whiteness in the Absence of Wages: Racial Capitalism, Reactionary Intercommunalism and the Rise of Trumpism', *Third World Quarterly*, 38:11 (2017): 2482–500.

82. *Sky News*, 'Home Secretary: "Not Racist" to Control Borders' (4 October 2022), news.sky.com/video/home-secretary-not-racist-to-control-borders-12712393, (last accessed November 2022).

83. Maya Goodfellow, 'Think Priti Patel Was Bad? Suella Braverman Wants to Make Claiming Asylum Near-Impossible', *Guardian* (5 October 2022), www.theguardian.com/commentisfree/2022/oct/05/priti-patel-suella-braverman-claiming-asylum-home-secretary, (last accessed November 2022).

84. Jessica Elgot, 'England's Tyrone Mings Criticises Priti Patel Over Racism Remarks', *Guardian* (13 July 2021), www.theguardian.com/politics/2021/jul/13/england-tyrone-mings-criticises-priti-patel-over-racism-remarks, (last accessed November 2022).

85. Jasmin Gray, 'Priti Patel: I've Been Racially Abused in the Street – Don't Lecture Me About Inequality', *Huffington Post* (8 June 2020), www.huffingtonpost.co.uk/entry/priti-patel-florence-eshalomi-racial-inequality_uk_5ede663ec5b6cfa4c5a9d82e, (last accessed November 2022).

86. Benjamin Lynch, 'Rishi Sunak's Massive Net Worth and Marriage to Billionaire Wife Who's Richer than the Queen', *The Mirror* (12 April 2022), www.mirror.co.uk/news/politics/inside-lavish-life-rishi-sunak-25310064, (last accessed November 2022).

87. Mared Gruffydd, 'Priti Patel Net Worth: How Much Money Does the Home Secretary Have, *Daily Express* (15 March 2021), www.express.co.uk/life-style/life/1387559/priti-patel-net-worth, (last accessed November 2022).

88. Will Hayward, 'The Wealthiest Ministers in the UK Government Cabinet', *Wales Online* (12 April 2022), www.walesonline.co.uk/news/wales-news/wealthiest-ministers-uk-government-cabinet-23666390, (accessed November 2022).

89. Mared Gruffydd, 'Priti Patel Net Worth'.

90. Ilyas Nagdee and Azfar Shafi, Prime Minister Rishi Sunak is Not a Victory for Anti-racism', *Dazed* (25 October 2022), www.dazeddigital.com/life-culture/article/57288/1/prime-minister-rishi-sunak-is-not-a-victory-for-anti-racism, (last accessed December 2022).

91. BBC, 'Nusrat Ghani: Muslimness a Reason for My Sacking, Says Ex-minister', (23 January 2022), www.bbc.co.uk/news/uk-politics-60100525, (accessed October 2022).
92. Simon Murphy, 'Sayeeda Warsi on Tory Islamophobia: "It Feels Like I'm in an Abusive Relationship"', *Guardian* (27 November 2019), www.theguardian.com/politics/2019/nov/27/sayeeda-warsi-tory-islamophobia-muslim-prejudice-investigation, (accessed November 2022).
93. Home Office, *Revised Prevent Duty Guidance for England and Wales* (London: HM Govt, 2021), www.gov.uk/government/publications/prevent-duty-guidance/revised-prevent-duty-guidance-for-england-and-wales, (last accessed December 2022).
94. Jamie Grierson, 'Hostile Environment: Anatomy of a Policy Disaster'.
95. Luke De Noronha, *Deporting Black Britons* (Manchester: Manchester University Press, 2020), p. 148.
96. Nadine El-Enany, *Bordering Britain* (Manchester: Manchester University Press, 2020), p. 4.
97. WBG, 'WBG Warns Against Austerity 2.0, a Triple Whammy For Women', press release (14 November 2022), wbg.org.uk/media/wbg-warns-against-austerity-2-0-a-triple-whammy-for-women/, (last accessed November 2022).

## Chapter One

1. Belfast Telegraph, 'Thatcher Raps Muslim Response to Terror Attacks', (5 July 2008), www.belfasttelegraph.co.uk/imported/thatcher-raps-muslim-response-to-terror-attacks-28272387.html, (last accessed December 2022).
2. HM Government, *Countering International Terrorism: The United Kingdom's Strategy* (London: HMSO, July 2006, CM6888), assets.publishing.service.gov.uk/government/uploads/system/uploads/attachment_data/file/272320/6888.pdf, (accessed December 2022), p. 6.
3. William Wilson Hunter, *The Indian Musalmans: Are They Bound in Conscience to Rebel Against the Queen?* (London: Trübner & Co, 1872), p. 10.
4. Richard Taylor-Norton, 'MI5 and 7/7: A Matter of Resources Not Powers, Just Like Today', *Guardian* (6 July 2015), www.theguardian.com/news/defence-and-security-blog/2015/jul/06/mi5-and-77-a-matter-of-resources-not-powers-just-like-today, (accessed June 2022).
5. HM Government, *Countering International Terrorism*, p. 1.
6. Ibid.

7.  European Monitoring Centre on Racism and Xenophobia, *The Impact of 7 July 2005 London Bomb Attacks on Muslim communities in the EU* (November 2005),_fra.europa.eu/sites/default/files/fra_uploads/197-London-Bomb-attacks-EN.pdf, (accessed July 2022), p. 20.

8.  Shiv Malik, 'My Brother the Bomber', *Prospect* (30 June 2007), www.prospectmagazine.co.uk/magazine/my-brother-the-bomber-mohammad-sidique-khan (accessed June 2022).

9.  Ibid.

10. Ibid.

11. Sivamohan Valluvan, *The Clamour of Nationalism* (Manchester: Manchester University Press, 2019), p. 71.

12. Ibid, p. 72.

13. Ted Cantle, *Community Cohesion: A Report of the Independent Review Team*, (London: HM Government, Home Office, 2001), tedcantle.co.uk/pdf/communitycohesion%20cantlereport.pdf, (accessed June 2022).

14. Ibid.

15. Malik, 'My Brother the Bomber'.

16. Ibid.

17. Ibid.

18. 'Prime Minister Blair's Speech', *New York Times* (16 July 2005), www.nytimes.com/2005/07/16/international/europe/prime-minister-blairs-speech.html, (accessed June 2022).

19. Ibid.

20. Karyn Kusama, *The Invitation* (Darkhouse Pictures, 2015).

21. Ibid.

22. The MCB, 'About Us', mcb.org.uk/about/, (accessed June 2022).

23. Jonathan Birt, 'Lobbying and Marching: British Muslims and the State', in *Muslim Britain: Communities Under Pressure* (London: Zed Books, 2005): 92–106, here p. 93.

24. Ibid, p. 99.

25. Ibid.

26. HM Government, *Preventing Extremism Together Working Groups* (London, HMSO, 2006), p. 3.

27. Ibid.

28. 'Trevor Phillips Suspended from Labour Over Alleged Islamophobia', *al Jazeera* (9 March 2020), www.aljazeera.com/news/2020/3/9/trevor-phillips-suspended-from-labour-over-alleged-islamophobia, (accessed June 2022).

29. Haroon Siddique, 'Labour Lifts Trevor Phillips' Suspension for Alleged Islamophobia', *Guardian* (6 July 2021), www.theguardian.com/

uk-news/2021/jul/06/labour-lifts-trevor-phillips-suspension-for-alleged-islamophobia, (accessed June 2022).

30. Ibid.
31. Apsana Begum, twitter.com/apsanabegummp/status/141238827 8305705989?lang=en-GB. (accessed June 2022).
32. Martyn Frampton, , John Jenkins and Khalid Mahmood, 'The Trial: The Strange Case of Trevor Phillips', *Policy Exchange* (8 March 2020), https:// policyexchange.org.uk/publication/the-trial-the-strange-case-of-trevor-phillips/ (accessed January 2023).
33. Ibid.
34. Aditya Chakraborrty, 'Keir Starmer, Your Party Has a Whole New Race Problem', *Guardian* (7 July 2021), www.theguardian.com/ commentisfree/2021/jul/07/keir-starmer-labour-muslim-voters-red-wall-islamophobia, (accessed June 2022).
35. Brian Drohan, *Brutality in an Age of Human Rights: Activism and Counterinsurgency at the End of the British Empire* (New York: Cornell University Press, 2018).
36. Kim Wagner, 'Savage Warfare: Violence and the Rule of Colonial Difference in Early British Counterinsurgency', *History Workshop Journal*, 85(3) (2018): 217–37, p. 221.
37. Ibid, p. 218.
38. Rizwaan Sabir, 'Blurred Lines and False Dichotomies: Integrating Counterinsurgency into the UK's Domestic "War on Terror"' *Critical Social Policy*, 37(2) (2017): 202–24.
39. Ibid.
40. Alan Lester, Kate Boehme and Peter Mitchell, *Ruling the World; Freedom, Civilisation and Liberalism in the Nineteenth Century British Empire* (Cambridge: Cambridge University Press, 2021), p. 222.
41. Ibid.
42. Ibid.
43. Priyamvada Gopal, *Insurgent Empire* (London: Verso, 2019), p. IX.
44. Wagner, *Savage Warfare*, p. 220.
45. Gopal, *Insurgent Empire*, p. 49.
46. Ibid, p. 48.
47. Alex Padamsee, *Representations of Indian Muslims in British Colonial Discourse* (Basingstoke: Palgrave Macmillan, 2005).
48. Ibid, p. 56.
49. Ibid, p. 57.
50. Ibid, p. 63.
51. Ibid, p. 53.
52. Ibid, p. 50.

53. Ibid, p. 83.
54. William Wilson Hunter, *The Indian Musalmans: Are They Bound in Conscience to Rebel Against the Queen?* (London: Turner and Company, 1871), p. 11.
55. HM Government, *Countering International Terrorism: The United Kingdom's Strategy* (London: HMSO, 2006), p. 1.
56. Jessica Elgot and Vikram Dodd, 'Leaked Prevent Review Attacks "Double Standards" on Far Right and Islamists', *Guardian* (16 May 2022), www.theguardian.com/uk-news/2022/may/16/leaked-prevent-review-attacks-double-standards-on-rightwingers-and-islamists#:~:text=In%20Shawcross's%20draft%20review%20of,is%20not%20being%20sufficiently%20met%E2%80%9D, (accessed June 2022).
57. Walter Reich's (1990) *Origins of Terrorism: Psychologies, Ideologies, Theologies and States of Mind* (Cambridge: Cambridge University Press) provides a useful overview of the key debates in Terrorism Studies prior to 9/11. Chapters from Franco Ferracuti ('Ideology and repentance') and Konrad Kellen ('Ideology and Rebellion: Terrorism in West Germany') shed light on the prevalence of personal/psychological explanations like narcissism and trauma for terrorism.
58. Magnus Ranstorp, 'Introduction', in *Understanding Violent Radicalisation: Terrorist and Jihadist Movements Europe*, ed. Magnus Ranstorp (Abingdon: Routledge, 2010):1–19, p. 1.
59. Lisa Stampnitzsky, *Disciplining Terror: How Experts Invented "Terrorism"* (Cambridge: Cambridge University Press, 2013).
60. HM Government, *Countering International Terrorism*, p. 1.
61. Mary J. Hickman et al., *Suspect Communities'? Counter-terrorism policy, the press, and the impact on Irish and Muslim communities in Britain*, ESRC RES-062-23-1066 (London: London Metropolitan University, 2011).
62. Arun Kundnani, *The Muslims Are Coming! Islamophobia, Extremism, and the Domestic War on Terror* (London: Verso, 2014), p. 117.
63. HM Government, *Contest: the United Kingdom's Strategy for Countering Terrorism* (London: HMSO, 2009), p. 15.
64. Salman Sayyid, 'Answering the Muslim question: The Politics of Muslims in Europe', *e-cadernos CES [Online]*, 3, journals.openedition.org/eces/180, (last accessed December 2022).
65. Salman Sayyid and AbdoolKarim Vakil, 'Defining Islamophobia', *Critical Muslim Studies* (5 December 2019), criticalmuslimstudies.co.uk/project/defining-islamophobia/, (accessed December 2022).
66. Farid Hafez, 'Converging Islamophobias in Europe: The Visegrad Four Countries and Their Western "Forerunners"', *The Maydan*, (30th November 2017), https://themaydan.com/2017/11/converging-

islamophobias-europe-visegrad-four-countries-western-forerunners/ (accessed February 2023).

67. Talal Assad, 'The Idea of an Anthropology of Islam', Que Parle, 17(2) (2009): 1–30, https://doi.org/10.5250/quiparle.17.2.1.

*Chapter Two*

1. Sara Cannizzaro and Reza Gholami, 'The Devil is Not in the Detail: Representational Absence and Stereotyping in the "Trojan Horse" News Story', *Race, Ethnicity and Education*, 21(1) (2018): 15–29.
2. For more details, you can listen to the Trojan Horse Affair podcast by Hamza Syed and Brian Reed.
3. Michael Gove, *Celsius 7/7* (London: Weidenfeld & Nicolson, 2006).
4. Richard Adams, 'Trojan Horse School Damned in Ofsted Report', *Guardian* (6 June 2014), www.theguardian.com/education/2014/jun/06/trojan-horse-school-ofsted-report-park-view, (accessed June 2022).
5. Peter Clarke, 'Report into Allegations Concerning Birmingham Schools Arising from the 'Trojan Horse' Letter', (July 2014), assets.publishing. service.gov.uk/government/uploads/system/uploads/attachment_data/file/340526/HC_576_accessible_-.pdf, (accessed June 2022).
6. Adams, 'Trojan Horse School Damned in Ofsted Report'.
7. Ghassan Hage, 'The Spatial Imaginary of National Practices: Dwelling— Domesticating /Being—Exterminating', *Environment and Planning D: Society and Space*, 14(4) (1996): 463–85, here p. 479.
8. Ghassan Hage, *White Nation: Fantasies of White Supremacy in a Multicultural Society* (Melbourne: Routledge in association with Pluto Press Australia, 2000).
9. Clarke, 'Report into Allegations Concerning Birmingham Schools', p. 8.
10. Department for Communities and Local Government, *Preventing Violent Extremism Pathfinder Fund Mapping of Project Activities 2007/2008* (London: Communities and Local Government Publications, 2008), p. 24.
11. Cindi John, 'Imams Hit Road to Beat Extremism', *BBC* (15 February 2006), http://news.bbc.co.uk/2/hi/uk_news/4710096.stm (accessed June 2022).
12. Sergei Prozorov, *Political Pedagogy of Technical Assistance* (University of Tampere: Department of Political Science and IR, 2004).
13. HM Government, *The Prevent Strategy: A Guide for Local Partners in England* (London: HMSO, 2007), p. 18.
14. Ibid., p. 22.
15. Ibid.

16. Ibid.
17. Bernard Crick, *Education for Citizenship and the Teaching of Democracy in Schools, Citizenship Advisory Board* (London: Qualifications and Curriculum Authority, 1998).
18. Ibid, p. 17.
19. House of Commons Education and Skills Committee, *Education and Skills – Second Report* (London: HMSO, 2007), publications.parliament.uk/pa/cm200607/cmselect/cmeduski/147/14702.htm, (accessed June 2022).
20. Sivamohan Valluvan, (2019) *The Clamour of Nationalism: Race and Nation in Twenty First Century Britain,* (Manchester: Manchester University Press, 2019).
21. Rob B. J. Walker, *Inside/Outside; International Relations as Political Theory* (Cambridge, Cambridge University Press, 1992).
22. Maurice I. Coles, *When Hope and History Rhyme* (Leicester: The ICE Project, 2010), p. 4.
23. Ibid, p. 10.
24. Ibid.
25. Ibid.
26. Ibid.
27. Ben Kisby, '"Politics is Ethics Done in Public": Exploring Linkages and Disjunctions between Citizenship Education and Character Education in England', *Journal of Social Science Education,* 16(3) (2017): 8–20, here p. 10.
28. Ibid.
29. HM Government, *Tackling Extremism in the UK* (London: Cabinet Office, 2013), p. 1.
30. R. Harris, 'British Values, Citizenship and the Teaching of History', in I. Davies (ed.), *Debates in History Teaching* (Routledge, Abingdon, 2017), pp. 180–90.
31. Hugh Starkey, 'Fundamental British Values and Citizenship Education: Tensions Between National and Global Perspectives', *Geografiska Annaler: Series B, Human Geography,* 100(2) (2018): 149–62, here p. 149.
32. Ibid, p. 152.
33. Christine Winter and China Mills, 'The Psy-Security-Curriculum Ensemble: British Values Curriculum Policy in English Schools', *Journal of Education Policy,* 35(1) (2020): 46–67, here p. 56.
34. Gopal, *Insurgent Empire.*
35. Claire Crawford, 'Promoting "Fundamental British Values" in Schools: A Critical Race Perspective', *Curriculum Perspectives,* 37 (2017): 197–204, here p. 199.

36. Lawrence Archer and Fiona Bawdon, *Ricin! The Inside Story of the Terror Plot That Never Was* (London: Pluto Press, 2010), p. 4.
37. UK Department of Defence, *JTF-GTMO Detainee Assessment: Nabil Said Hadjarab*, 2007, WikiLeaks: the Guantanamo http://wikileaks.org/gitmo/pdf/ag/us9ag-000238dp.pdf, (accessed June 2022).
38. Sophie Gilliat-Ray, *Muslims in Britain* (Cambridge: Cambridge University Press, 2010), p. 182.
39. MINAB, 'About Us', minab.org.uk/about-us/, (accessed June 2022).
40. HM Treasury, *Corporate Governance in Central Government Departments: A Code of Best Practice*, (London: HMSO, 2011).
41. Randeep Ramesh, 'Quarter of Charity Commission Inquiries Target Muslim Groups', *Guardian* (16 November 2014), www.theguardian.com/society/2014/nov/16/charity-commission-inquiries-muslim-groups, (accessed June 2022).
42. Urban Nexus and MINAB, *Beacon Mosques Programme* (St Albans: Urban Nexus, 2010), p. 2.
43. Ibid, p. 5.
44. Shaukat Warraich and Kashaff Feroze, A Management Guide for Mosques and Islamic Centres (Oldham: Faith Associates, 2007), www.faithassociates.co.uk/wp-content/uploads/2018/03/faith-associates-mosque-management-toolkit-fa-uk.pdf.
45. Ifath Nawaz and Shaukat Warraich, *Mosques and Imams National Advisory Board Consultation, Findings and Conclusion* (Oldham: Faith Associates, 2006), pp. 6–7.
46. MINAB, (2007) *The Mosques in the Communities Project: Understanding the Role of Mosques in Relation to their Local Communities*, https://www.faith-matters.org/wp-content/uploads/2011/09/the-mosques-in-communities-project.pdf, p. 8.
47. Naaz Rashid, *Veiled Threats; Representing the Muslim Woman in Public Policy Discourse* (Bristol: Policy Press, 2016).
48. Rashid, *Veiled Threats*, p. 161.
49. Martin van Bruinessen and Stefano Allievi, *Producing Islamic Knowledge: Transmission and dissemination in Western Europe* (Abingdon: Routledge, 2011), p. 7.
50. Sophie Gilliat-Ray, Mansur Ali and Stephen Pattinson, *Understanding Muslim Chaplaincy*, (Farnham: Ashgate, 2013), p. 5.
51. Ibid, p. 7.
52. Jonathan Birt, 'Good Imam, Bad Imam: Civic Religion and National Integration Post-9/11', *The Muslim World*, 96(4) (2006): 687–705, p. 687, https://doi.org/10.1111/j.1478-1913.2006.00153.x.
53. HM Government, *Prevent Strategy*, (London: HMSO, 2011).

NOTES

54. Ibid, p. 6.

55. Shiraz Maher Martyn Frampton, *Choosing our Friends Wisely: Criteria for Engagement with Muslim Groups* (London: Policy Exchange, 2009), policyexchange.org.uk/wp-content/uploads/2016/09/choosing-our-friends-wisely-mar-09.pdf. (accessed June 2022).

56. David Cameron, 'PM's Speech at Munich Security Conference', Munich, 5 February 2011, www.gov.uk/government/speeches/pms-speech-at-munich-security-conference, (accessed June 2022).

57. Lester, Boehme and Mitchell, *Ruling the World*, p. 8.

58. Ibid.

59. Hilary Aked, *False Positives: The Prevent Counter-Extremism Policy in Healthcare*, (London: Medact, 2020), p .27.

60. Ibid.

61. Shereen Fernandez, Rob. F Walker and Tarek Younis, 'The "Where" of Prevent', *Discover Society*, (6 April 2018), archive.discoversociety.org/2018/06/05/focus-the-where-of-prevent/, (accessed June 2022).

62. Aked, *False Positives*, p. 5.

63. Ibid.

64. Tarek Younis and Sushrat Jadav, 'Keeping Our Mouths Shut: The Fear and Racialized Self-Censorship of British Healthcare Professionals in PREVENT Training', *Culture, Medicine, and Psychiatry*, 43 (2019): 404–24.

65. Ibid.

## Chapter Three

1. Cited in David Anderson Q.C., *Citizenship Removal Resulting in Statelessness* (London: HMSO, 2016).

2. Nisha Kapoor, *Deport, Deprive, Extradite: 21st Century State Extremism*, (London: Verso, 2018).

3. Good Law Project, 'The Nationality and Borders Bill Is Racist – We Want Government to Think Again', (18 January 2022), goodlawproject.org/news/nationality-borders-bill-clause-9/, (accessed June 2022).

4. C. J. McKinney, 'How Many People Have Been Stripped of Their British citizenship?', *Free Movement Organisation* (10 January 2022), freemovement.org.uk/how-many-people-have-been-stripped-of-their-british-citizenship-home-office-deprivation/, (accessed June 2022).

5. Salman Sayyid, 'A Measure of Islamophobia', *Islamophobia Studies Journal*, 2(1) (2014): 10–25.

6. BBC, 'Nusrat Ghani: Muslimness a Reason for My Sacking, Says Ex-minister', (23 January 2022), www.bbc.co.uk/news/uk-politics-60100525, (accessed October 2022).

7.  Robert Booth, 'Tories Step Up Attempts to Link Sadiq Khan to Extremists', *Guardian* (20 April 2016), www.theguardian.com/politics/2016/apr/20/tory-claims-sadiq-khan-alleged-links-extremists, (accessed June 2022).
8.  Zac Goldsmith, 'On Thursday Are We Really Going to Hand the World's Greatest City to a Labour Party That Thinks Terrorists is [sic] its friends?', *Daily Mail* (1 May 2016), www.dailymail.co.uk/debate/article-3567537/On-Thursday-really-going-hand-world-s-greatest-city-Labour-party-thinks-terrorists-friends-passionate-plea-ZAC-GOLDSMITH-four-days-Mayoral-election.html, (accessed June 2022).
9.  Rebecca Flood, 'Imam DEMANDS Apology from David Cameron After Being Labelled ISIS Supporter', *Daily Express* (15 May 2016), www.express.co.uk/news/uk/667319/Imam-ISIS-David-Cameron-apology-Jeremy-Cobyn-supporter, (accessed June 2022).
10. Heather Stewart, 'David Cameron Apologises after Saying Ex-imam "Supported Islamic State"', *Guardian* (11 May 2016), www.theguardian.com/politics/2016/may/11/david-cameron-apologises-after-saying-ex-imam-supported-islamic-state, (accessed June 2022).
11. Mark Chandler, 'Londoners Reject Racist "London Has Fallen' Tweets with Messages of Unity After Sadiq Khan Victory', *Evening Standard* (7 May 2016), www.standard.co.uk/news/mayor/londoners-reject-racist-london-has-fallen-tweets-with-messages-of-unity-after-sadiq-khan-victory-a3242526.html, (accessed June 2022).
12. Lee Jarvis, and Michael Lister, *Anti-Terrorism, Citizenship and Security* (Manchester: Manchester University Press, 2015), p. 6.
13. Engin Isin, *Being Political: Genealogies of Citizenship* (Minnesota: University of Minnesota Press, 2002), p. 1.
14. Immanuel Wallerstein, 'Citizens All? Citizens Some! The Making of the Citizen', *Comparative Studies in Society and History*, 45(4) (2003): 650–79, here p. 652.
15. Ibid.
16. Roger Brubaker, 'The French Revolution and the Invention of Citizenship', *French Politics and Society*, 7(3) (1989): 30–49, here p. 38.
17. Jack Harrington, 'Orientalism, Political Subjectivity and the Birth of Citizenship between 1780 and 1830', in Engin Isin (ed.), *Citizenship After Orientalism: Citizenship: Transforming Political Theory* (Basingstoke: Palgrave Macmillan, 2014), p. 59.
18. Engin Isin, 'Transforming Political Theory', in Engin Isin (ed.), *Citizenship After Orientalism*, pp. 1–2.
19. Barry Hindess, 'Postcolonial Citizenship in the Empire', in Thomas Blom Hansen and Finn Stepputat (eds), *Sovereign Bodies: Citizens, Migrants, and*

*States in the Postcolonial World* (New Jersey: Princeton University Press, 2005), pp. 241–56.

20. Cameron, 'PM's speech at Munich Security Conference'.
21. Ibid.
22. Naaz Rashid, *Veiled Threats* (Bristol: Policy Press, 2016).
23. Jasmine Zine, 'Unveiled Sentiments: Gendered Islamophobia and Experiences of Veiling among Muslim Girls in a Canadian Islamic School', *Equity and Excellence in Education*, 39(3) (2006): 239–55.
24. Lila Abu-Lughod, 'Do Muslim Women Really Need Saving? Anthropological Reflections on Cultural Relativism and Its Others', *American Anthropologist*, 104(3) (2002): 783–90.
25. Gargi Bhattacharyya, *Dangerous Brown Men: Exploiting Sex, Violence and Feminism in the 'War on Terror'* (London: Zed Books, 2007), p. 24.
26. Crown Prosecution Service, 'So-Called Honour-Based Abuse and Forced Marriage', (updated 26 September 2019), www.cps.gov.uk/legal-guidance/so-called-honour-based-abuse-and-forced-marriage., (accessed June 2022).
27. Rashid, *Veiled Threats*, p. xi.
28. Ibid.
29. Department for Communities and Local Government, *Empowering Muslim Women: Case Studies* (West Yorkshire: Communities and Local Government Publications, 2008), dera.ioe.ac.uk/7422/7/669801_Redacted.pdf, (accessed June 2022), p. 2.
30. Rashid, *Veiled Threats*, p. 96.
31. Ibid.
32. Ibid.
33. Rashid, *Veiled Threats*, p. 101.
34. For details of Inspire's work see: www.sarakhan.co.uk/.
35. Inspire, 'About Inspire', *YouTube* (29 September 2014), www.youtube.com/watch?v=m7TNWXoet1s, (accessed June 2022).
36. Ibid.
37. Roy Greenslade, '*The Sun* Makes a Bold Bid to Prevent Brits Becoming Isis Recruits', *Guardian* (8 October 2014), www.theguardian.com/media/greenslade/2014/oct/08/sun-isis (accessed June 2022).
38. Inspire, 'Making a Stand in Leeds', *YouTube* (2 April 2015), www.youtube.com/watch?v=FKGQp_ApEBE, (accessed June 2022).
39. Inspire, 'Making a Stand in Cardiff', *YouTube* (2 April 2015), www.youtube.com/watch?v=qOYlotbok7c, (accessed June 2022).
40. Inspire, 'Making a Stand in West London', *YouTube* (2 April 2015), www.youtube.com/watch?v=TKXLbFZ6cio, (accessed June 2022).

41. Inspire, 'Making a Standing in Leeds', *YouTube* (2 April 2015), www.youtube.com/watch?v=FKGQp_ApEBE, (accessed June 2022).

42. Inspire, 'Making a Stand in East London', *YouTube* (2 April 2015), https://www.youtube.com/watch?v=LFXkwNv2mZY&ab_channel=WeWillInspire, (accessed June 2022).

43. Inspire, 'Making a Stand in Cardiff'.

44. Inspire, '#MakingAStand Launch: Speeches from Sara Khan and Others', *YouTube* (1 October 2014), www.youtube.com/watch?v=2F6T3tFL_O4&t=565s, (accessed June 2022).

45. Katarzyna Falecka, 'From Colonial Algeria to Modern Day Europe, the Muslim Veil Remains an Ideological Battleground', *The Conversation* (24 January 2017), theconversation.com/from-colonial-algeria-to-modern-day-europe-the-muslim-veil-remains-an-ideological-battleground-70242, (accessed June 2022).

46. Mark Townsend, 'Muslim Boy, 4, Was Referred to Prevent Over Game of *Fortnite*', *Guardian* (31 January 2021), www.theguardian.com/uk-news/2021/jan/31/muslim-boy-4-was-referred-to-prevent-over-game-of-fortnite, (accessed June 2022).

47. Ben Quinn, 'Nursery "Raised Fears of Radicalisation Over Boy's Cucumber Drawing"', *Guardian* (11 March 2016), www.theguardian.com/uk-news/2016/mar/11/nursery-radicalisation-fears-boys-cucumber-drawing-cooker-bomb, (accessed June 2022).

48. Diane Taylor, 'Boy, 11, Referred to Prevent for Wanting to Give "Alms to the Oppressed"', *Guardian* (27 June 2021), www.theguardian.com/uk-news/2021/jun/27/boy-11-referred-to-prevent-for-wanting-to-give-alms-to-the-oppressed, (accessed June 2022).

49. Ibid.

50. Jamie Grierson, 'Counter-terror Police Running Secret Prevent Database', *Guardian* (6 October 2019), www.theguardian.com/uk-news/2019/oct/06/counter-terror-police-are-running-secret-prevent-database, (accessed June 2022).

51. Nadya Ali, 'Writing for the Kids', in Asim Qureshi (ed.), *I Refuse to Condemn: Resisting Racism in Time of National Security* (Manchester: Manchester University Press, 2020), p.164.

52. Phillip A. Goff et al., (2014) The Essence of Innocence: Consequences of Dehumanizing Black Children, *Journal of Personality and Social Psychology*, 106:4 (2014): 526–45, here p. 526.

53. Rebecca Epstein, Jamilia J. Blake and Thalia González, *Girlhood Interrupted: The Erasure of Black Girls' Childhood* (Washington DC: Georgetown Law Center on Poverty and Inequality, 2017),

genderjusticeandopportunity.georgetown.edu/wp-content/uploads/
2020/06/girlhood-interrupted.pdf, (accessed June 2022).
54. Ibid.
55. Save the Children, *More than 60 British Children Trapped in North East Syria* (London: Save the Children, 2021), www.savethechildren.org.uk/
news/media-centre/press-releases/More-than-60-British-children-
trapped-in-North-East-Syria, (accessed June 2022).
56. Andrei Popoviciu, 'Syria: UK Repatriates Three British Children from Islamic State Camps', *Middle East Eye* (19 October 2021), www.
middleeasteye.net/news/uk-syria-children-repatriation-islamic-state-
camps, (accessed June 2022).
57. Melanie Newman, 'Preventing Far Right Extremism? Schools in EDL and BNP Heartlands Only Monitoring Ethnic Minority Pupils', *The Bureau of Investigative Journalism* (31 March 2015), www.thebureauinvestigates.
com/stories/2015-03-31/preventing-far-right-extremism-schools-in-edl-
and-bnp-heartland-only-monitoring-ethnic-minority-pupils, (accessed June 2022).
58. MCB, 'Meeting Between David Anderson QC and MCB: Concerns on Prevent' (28 July 2015), http://archive.mcb.org.uk/wp-content/
uploads/2015/10/20150803-Case-studies-about-Prevent.pdf, (accessed January 2023).
59. Lee Jerome, Alex Elwick and Raza Kazim, 'The Impact of the Prevent Duty on Schools: What Does the Evidence Tell Us?', *British Educational Research Association* (2 July 2019), www.bera.ac.uk/blog/the-impact-of-
the-prevent-duty-on-schools-what-does-the-evidence-tell-us, (accessed June 2022).
60. Alex Elwick, Lee Jerome and Hans Svennevig, 'Student Perspectives on Teaching and Prevent Policy', in Joel Busher and Lee Jerome (eds), *The Prevent Duty in Education: Impact, Enactment and Implications*, (Basingstoke: Palgrave Macmillan, 2020): 55–76, p. 61.

## Chapter Four

1. Amrit Wilson, *Finding a Voice: Asian Women in Britain* (Québec: Qaraja Press, [1978] 2018).
2. Sean Morrison, 'Nigel Farage Visited by Police Over "Breaching Lockdown" by Travelling to Dover to Report on Migrants', *The Standard* (4 May 2020), www.standard.co.uk/news/uk/nigel-farage-visited-by-
police-over-lockdown-breaches-over-dover-travel-a4431871.html,
(accessed 2020).

3. Rachel Hall, 'RNLI Hits Out at "Migrant Taxi Service" Accusations', *Guardian* (28 July 2021), www.theguardian.com/uk-news/2021/jul/28/rnli-hits-out-migrant-taxi-service-accusations, (accessed June 2022).
4. In December 2022, four migrants died in their attempts to cross the English Channel. This followed the deaths of 27 migrants making the same journey in November 2021. On both occasions the home secretaries Priti Patel and Suella Braverman, respectively, bemoaned the tragic deaths, while nevertheless placing the focus on smugglers and strengthening punitive immigration laws. Patel's response can be found here: www.gov.uk/government/speeches/home-secretarys-speech-on-channel-drownings, (accessed December 2022) and Braverman's here: www.theguardian.com/politics/2022/dec/14/suella-braverman-says-uk-must-end-these-crossings-after-channel-deaths, (accessed December 2022).
5. Maya Goodfellow, *Hostile Environment* (London: Verso, 2019), p. 97.
6. Ibid, p. 96.
7. Ibid.
8. The Conservative Party Manifesto, 2015: general-election-2010.co.uk/2010-general-election-manifestos/Conservative-Party-Manifesto-2010.pdf, (accessed June 2022).
9. Hannah Jones et al., *Go Home? The Politics of Immigration Controversies* (Manchester: Manchester University Press, 2017), p. 11
10. Ibid, p. 3.
11. Alan Travis, 'Immigration Bill: Theresa May Defends Plans to Create "Hostile Environment"', *Guardian* (10 October 2013), www.theguardian.com/politics/2013/oct/10/immigration-bill-theresa-may-hostile-environment, (accessed June 2022).
12. Ian Sanjay Patel, *We're Here Because You Were There; Immigration and the End of Empire* (London: Verso Books, 2021), pp. 6–7.
13. John Solomos, *Race and Racism in Britain* (Basingstoke: Palgrave Macmillan, 1989).
14. Armağan Teke Lloyd, *Exclusion and Inclusion in International Migration: Power, Resistance and Identity* (London: Transnational Press, 2019), p. 6.
15. Matthew Weaver, 'The Gordon Brown and Gillian Duffy Transcript', *Guardian* (28 April 2010), www.theguardian.com/politics/2010/apr/28/gordon-brown-gillian-duffy-transcript, (accessed June 2022).
16. Ibid.
17. Amelia Gentleman, *The Windrush Betrayal*, (London: Guardian Faber, 2019), p. 120.
18. 'Howard Vows to Reform or Scrap Human Rights Act', *The Times* (18 March 2005), www.thetimes.co.uk/article/howard-vows-to-reform-or-scrap-human-rights-act-bjvzfgtc5wd, (accessed June 2022).

19. Barbar Ahmed, 'When Prime Minister Theresa May Gloated at My Extradition', (13 July 2016), babarahmad.com/2016/07/13/when-prime-minister-theresa-may-gloated-at-my-extradition/, (accessed June 2022).
20. The Conservative Party Manifesto, 2015, p. 14.
21. Allison Pearson, 'Allison Pearson: We Must Get Rid of the Dreadful Human Rights Act', *Telegraph* (13 May 2015), www.telegraph.co.uk/news/uknews/law-and-order/11602222/Allison-Pearson-We-must-get-rid-of-the-dreadful-Human-Rights-Act.html, (accessed June 2022).
22. James Slack, 'End of Human Rights Farce: In a Triumphant Week for British Values, Tories Unveil Plans to Give Parliament and Judges Power to IGNORE the European Court and its Crazy Decisions', *Daily Mail* (3 October 2014), www.dailymail.co.uk/news/article-2778720/End-human-rights-farce-In-triumphant-week-British-values-Tories-unveil-plans-Parliament-judges-power-ignore-European-Court-crazy-decision-making.html, (accessed June 2022).
23. Decca Aitkenhead, 'Sarah Teather: "I'm Angry There Are No Alternative Voices on Immigration"', *Guardian* (12 July 2013), www.theguardian.com/theguardian/2013/jul/12/sarah-teather-angry-voices-immigration, (accessed June 2022).
24. Ibid.
25. Ibid.
26. David Laws, *Coalition Diaries 2012-2015,* (London: Biteback Publishing, 2017), p. 184.
27. Ibid, p. 43.
28. Ibid, p. 128.
29. Ibid.
30. Ibid.
31. 'Labour Backs Theresa May's Immigration Bill', *BBC* (22 October 2013), www.bbc.co.uk/news/uk-politics-24613222, (accessed June 2022).
32. Yvette Cooper, 'Let's Not Pretend That People Aren't Worried About Immigration', *Guardian* (28 May 2014), www.theguardian.com/commentisfree/2014/may/28/not-pretend-worried-immigration-ukip, (accessed June 2022).
33. Carlos Vargas-Silva, 'The Labour Market Effects of Immigration', *The Migration Observatory* (18 February 2020), migrationobservatory.ox.ac.uk/resources/briefings/the-labour-market-effects-of-immigration/, (accessed June 2022).
34. Satnam Virdee, *Racism, Class and the Racialized Outsider,* (London: Bloomsbury, 2014).
35. Ben Chu, 'Local Councils at Financial Breaking Point Due to Austerity, Warns National Audit Office, *Independent* (7 March 2018), www.

independent.co.uk/news/business/news/local-councils-finances-budget-cuts-austerity-services-national-audit-office-a8242556.html, (accessed June 2022).

36. Annette Hastings et al., *The Cost of the Cuts: The Impact on Local Government and Poorer Communities* (York: The Joseph Rowntree Foundation, 2015), www.jrf.org.uk/sites/default/files/jrf/migrated/files/Summary-Final.pdf, (accessed June 2022).

37. Vicki Cooper and David Whyte, *The Violence of Austerity* (London: Pluto Press, 2017).

38. 'Labour Has Changed on Immigration, Says Ed Miliband', *Guardian* (28 April 2015), www.theguardian.com/uk-news/2015/apr/28/labour-changed-immigration-ed-miliband-promise, (accessed January 2023).

39. Stephen Bush, 'Labour's Anti-immigrant Mug: The Worst Part Is, it Isn't a Gaffe', *The New Statesman* (28 March 2015), www.newstatesman.com/politics/2015/03/labours-anti-immigrant-mug-worst-part-it-isnt-gaffe, (accessed June 2022).

40. Laws, *Coalition Diaries 2012-2015*, p. 152.

41. Francis Webber, *The Embedding of State Hostility* (London: The Institute of Race Relations, 2018), irr.org.uk/app/uploads/2018/11/Embedding-State-hostility-v4.pdf, (accessed June 2022), p. 4.

42. Liberty (ed.), *A Guide to the Hostile Environment* (London: Liberty Human Rights, May 2018), www.libertyhumanrights.org.uk/wp-content/uploads/2020/02/Hostile-Environment-Guide-%E2%80%93-update-May-2019_0.pdf, (accessed June 2022), p. 38.

43. Home Office, *Tackling Illegal Immigration in Privately Rented Accommodation: The Government's response to the Consultation* (London: Home Office, October 2013), assets.publishing.service.gov.uk/government/uploads/system/uploads/attachment_data/file/249616/Consultation_Response.pdf, (accessed June 2022).

44. Ibid, p. 7.

45. Claire Brickell, Tom Bucke, Jonathan Burchell, et al., *Evaluation of the Right to Rent Scheme: Full Evaluation Report of Phase One* (London: Home Office, October 2015), assets.publishing.service.gov.uk/government/uploads/system/uploads/attachment_data/file/468934/horr83.pdf, (accessed June 2022), p. 8.

46. JCWI, *"No Passport Equals No Home": An Independent Evaluation of the "Right to Rent" Scheme* (London: Joint Council for the Welfare of Immigrants, 2015), jcwi.org.uk/sites/default/files/documets/No%20Passport%20Equals%20No%20Home%20Right%20to%20Rent%20Independent%20Evaluation_0.pdf, (accessed June 2020), p. 10.

47. Ibid, p. 10.

48. Brickell, Bucke, Burchell et al, *Evaluation of the Right to Rent Scheme*, p. 5.
49. David Bolt, *An Inspection of the "Right to Rent" Scheme*, Presented to Parliament pursuant to Section 50 (2) of the UK Borders Act 2007 March 2018 (London: HMSO, 2018) assets.publishing.service.gov.uk/government/uploads/system/uploads/attachment_data/file/695273/An_inspection_of_the_Right_to_Rent_scheme.pdf, (accessed June 2022), p. 42.
50. JCWI, *"No Passport Equals No Home"*, p. 55.
51. JCWI, *Passport Please: The Impact of the Right to Rent Checks on Migrants and Ethnic Minorities in England* (London: Joint Council for the Welfare of Immigrants, 2017), www.jcwi.org.uk/Handlers/Download.ashx?IDMF=ffcde3b5-e590-4b8e-931c-5ecf280e1bc8, (accessed June 2022), p. 5.
52. Fiona Bawdon, *Chasing Status: If Not British, Then What Am I?* (London: Legal Action Group, 2014), https://www.lag.org.uk/document-downloads/204756/chasing-status--if-not-british--then-what-am-i-, (accessed January 2023).
53. JCWI, *Right to Rent Checks Declared Unlawful: What Next?* (London: Joint Council for the Welfare of Immigrants, 2019), www.jcwi.org.uk/Handlers/Download.ashx?IDMF=7d9b4e89-d358-40a6-912b-f6bced549219, (accessed June 2022).
54. Samuel March, 'Government Successfully Appeals in "Right to Rent" Case', *UK Human Rights Blog* (22 April 2020), ukhumanrightsblog.com/2020/04/22/government-successfully-appeals-in-right-to-rent-case/, (accessed June 2022).
55. JCWI, *Passport Please*, p. 9.
56. Bolt, *An Inspection of the "Right to Rent" Scheme*.
57. Royal Courts of Justice, (2020) www.judiciary.uk/wp-content/uploads/2020/04/SSHD-v-JCWIfinal.pdf, (accessed June 2022).
58. HM Government, 'Penalties for Employing Illegal Workers', www.gov.uk/penalties-for-employing-illegal-workers, (accessed June 2022).
59. Ibid.
60. Ibid.
61. Diane Taylor, 'Fewer Than One in Six "Hostile Environment" Raids Led to Deportations', *Guardian* (21 February 2021), www.theguardian.com/uk-news/2021/feb/21/fewer-than-one-in-six-hostile-environment-raids-led-to-deportations, (accessed June 2022).
62. Jill Rennie, (2022) Immigration Raids on Care Homes During Lockdown Were "Irresponsible and Insensitive"', *Carehome.co.uk* (17 January 2022), www.carehome.co.uk/news/article.cfm/id/1663456/home-office-raids-care-homes, (accessed June 2022).

63. Amreen Qureshi, Marley Morris and Lucy Mort, *Access Denied: The Human Impact of the Hostile Environment* (London: IPPR, 2020), www.ippr.org/files/2020-09/access-denied-hostile-environment-sept20.pdf, (accessed June 2022), p. 7.

64. 'Northern Ireland Businesses Fined £1.3m for Employing Illegal Workers', *Belfast Telegraph* (19 July 2019), www.belfasttelegraph.co.uk/news/northern-ireland/northern-ireland-businesses-fined-13m-for-employing-illegal-workers-38327386.html, (accessed June 2022).

65. Isabel Shutes, *Social Care for Older People and Demand for Migrant Workers* (Oxford: The Migration Observatory, 2011), migrationobservatory.ox.ac.uk/wp-content/uploads/2016/04/Policy-Primer-Social-Care.pdf, (accessed June 2022).

66. Bee Wilson, 'Who Killed the Great British Curry House?', *Guardian* (12 January 2017), www.theguardian.com/lifeandstyle/2017/jan/12/who-killed-the-british-curry-house, (accessed June 2022).

67. Liberty, *A Guide to the Hostile Environment*, p. 19.

68. A. Kapilashrami et al., 'Ethnic Disparities in Health & Social Care Workers' Exposure, Protection, and Clinical Management of the COVID-19 Pandemic in the UK', *Critical Public Health*, 32(1) (2022): 68–81.

## Chapter Five

1. Alan Lester, *Deny and Disavow: Distancing the Imperial Past in the Culture Wars* (London: Sunrise Publishing, 2022).

2. Elsa Oommen, 'There Have Always Been a Hostile Environment', *Sociological Review* (November 2020), thesociologicalreview.org/magazine/november-2020/methodologies/there-have-always-been-a-hostile-environment/, (accessed June 2022).

3. Home Office, www.gov.uk/government/organisations/home-office, (accessed June 2022).

4. Luke De Noronha, *Deporting Black Britons* (Manchester University Press: Manchester, 2020); Nadine El-Enany, *Bordering Britain* (Manchester: Manchester University Press, 2020).

5. twitter.com/irr_news/status/1271126824093958150?lang=en, (accessed June 2022).

6. Ibid.

7. Ian Patel, *We're Here Because You Were There: Immigration and the End of Empire* (London: Verso Books, 2022).

8. Reiko Karatani, *Defining British Citizenship: Empire, Commonwealth and Modern Britain* (London: Frank Cass, 2003), p. 3.

9. Ibid, p. 4.

10. Ibid, p. 3.
11. Oommen, 'There Has Always Been a Hostile Environment'.
12. Luke De Noronha, *Deporting Black Britons* (Manchester University Press: Manchester, 2020), p. 147.
13. Ibid, p. 4.
14. Ibid, p. 5.
15. Ibid, p. 226.
16. Ibid, p. 148.
17. Leah Cowan, *Border Nation: A Story of Migration* (London: Pluto Press, 2020).
18. Ibid.
19. Ibid, p. 111.
20. Kamila Shamsie, 'Exiled: The Disturbing Story of a Citizen Made Unbritish', *Guardian* (17 November 2018), www.theguardian.com/books/2018/nov/17/unbecoming-british-kamila-shamsie-citizens-exile, (accessed June 2022).
21. Simon Hooper, 'EXCLUSIVE: Birmingham Aid Worker in Syria Stripped of UK Citizenship', *Middle East Eye* (21 May 2019), www.middleeasteye.net/news/exclusive-birmingham-aid-worker-syria-stripped-uk-citizenship, (accessed June 2022).
22. Dan Sabbagh, 'UK "Colluding in Torture" by Leaving Women and Children in Syria Camps', *Guardian* (13 October 2021), www.theguardian.com/world/2021/oct/13/uk-colluding-torture-leaving-women-children-syria-camps, (accessed June 2022).
23. Nigel Morris, 'A Control Order Ruined My Life – and My Respect for Britain', *Independent* (7 January 2011), www.independent.co.uk/news/uk/home-news/a-control-order-ruined-my-life-ndash-and-my-respect-for-britain-2178069.html, (accessed June 2022).
24. Alan Travis, 'Counter-terrorism Bill Will Enable "Internal Exile" of UK Suspects', *Guardian* (21 November 2014), www.theguardian.com/politics/2014/nov/21/counter-terrorism-bill-internal-exile-suspect-lib-dems-clegg, (accessed June 2022).
25. Amelia Gentleman, '"I Can't Eat or Sleep": The Woman Threatened with Deportation After 50 Years in Britain, *Guardian* (28 November 2017), www.theguardian.com/uk-news/2017/nov/28/i-cant-eat-or-sleep-the-grandmother-threatened-with-deportation-after-50-years-in-britain, (accessed June 2022).
26. Bawdon, *Chasing Status: If Not British, Then What Am I?*, p. 25.
27. Ibid.
28. Tom Gillespie, 'Windrush Scandal was "Foreseeable and Avoidable" – Report Finds', *Sky News* (19 March 2020), news.sky.com/story/

windrush-scandal-was-forseeable-and-avoidable-report-finds-11960256, (accessed June 2022).

29. Amelia Gentleman, 'Chased into "Self-Deportation": The Most Disturbing Windrush Case So Far', *Guardian* (14 September 2019), www.theguardian. com/uk-news/2019/sep/14/scale-misery-devastating-inside-story-reporting-windrush-scandal, (accessed June 2022).

30. Nadine El-Enany, *Bordering Britain* (Manchester: Manchester University Press, 2020).

31. Ibid, p. 4.

32. Ibid.

33. Ibid.

34. Ibid, p. 28.

35. Wendy Williams, *Windrush Lessons Learned Review* (March 2020), assets. publishing.service.gov.uk/government/uploads/system/uploads/ attachment_data/file/874022/6.5577_HO_Windrush_Lessons_ Learned_Review_WEB_v2.pdf, (accessed June 2022), p. 7.

36. Ibid, p. 7.

37. Ibid, p. 10.

38. Ibid, p. 13.

39. Rod Austin, 'Aid Worker Stranded in Syria After British Citizenship Revoked', *Guardian* (4 March 2019), www.theguardian.com/global-development/2019/mar/04/aid-worker-stranded-in-syria-after-british-citizenship-revoked, *Guardian*, (accessed June 2022).

40. Williams, *Windrush Lessons Learned Review*, p. 43.

41. Bawdon, *Chasing Status: If not British, then what am I?*.

42. Ibid.

43. Williams, *Windrush Lessons Learned Review*, p. 96.

44. Hazel Carby, *Imperial Intimacies: A Tale of Two Islands* (London: Verso Book, 2019).

45. Ibid, pp. 16–17.

46. Williams, *Windrush Lessons Learned Review*, p. 12.

47. Ibid.

48. Carby, *Imperial Intimacies: A Tale of Two Islands*, p. 12.

49. Justin Parkinson, 'UK Asylum Seekers "Told to Prove They Are Gay"', *BBC* (11 October 2013), www.bbc.co.uk/news/uk-politics-24479812, (accessed June 2022).

50. Geneva Abdul, 'Non-verbal Black Teenager Who Has Never Left UK Detained at Immigration Centre', *Guardian* (28 April 2022), www. theguardian.com/world/2022/apr/28/non-verbal-black-teenager-who-has-never-left-uk-detained-at-immigration-centre, (accessed June 2022).

# Conclusion

1. Francis Wade, 'Paul Gilroy: "Whiteness Just Ain't Worth What it Used to Be"', *The Nation* (8 October 2020), www.thenation.com/article/culture/paul-gilroy-interview/, (accessed June 2022).

2. Gargi Bhattacharyya et al., *Empire's Endgame: Racism and the British State* (London: Pluto Press, 2021).

3. Ibid, p. 2.

4. Sidney Jacobs, 'Race, Empire and the Welfare State: Council Housing and Racism', *Critical Social Policy*, 5(13) (1985): 6–28, doi:10.1177/026101838500501302.

5. Robert Rosenberg, *Rebel Footprints; A Guide to Uncovering London's Radical History* (London: Pluto Press, 2019).

6. Valluvan, *The Clamour of Nationalism*, p. 156.

7. Kojo Koram, *Uncommonwealth Wealth; Britain and the Aftermath of Empire* (London: John Murray, 2022), p. 6.

8. Ibid, p. 4.

9. Bhattacharyya et al, *Empire's Endgame*, p. 2.

10. Danny Dorling, Brexit, the NHS and the elderly middle class, *Soundings* (January 2017): 50–53, https://www.dannydorling.org/wp-content/files/dannydorling_publication_id5869.pdf, (accesses January 2023).

11. Gilroy, *There Ain't no Black in the Union Jack*, p. xxxii.

12. Ibid.

13. Marina Hyde, 'From the Government That Achieves Next to Nothing, it's The Rwanda Flight to Nowhere', *Guardian* (15 June 2022), www.theguardian.com/commentisfree/2022/jun/15/trump-wall-rwanda-deportation-flight-metaphor, (accessed June 2022).

# Index

Thanks to our Patreon subscriber:

*Ciaran Kane*

Who has shown generosity and
comradeship in support of our publishing.

Check out the other perks you get by subscribing
to our Patreon – visit patreon.com/plutopress.

Subscriptions start from £3 a month.